W9-BVI-593

HEAD OVER HEART IN LOVE: 25 GUIDES TO RATIONAL PASSION

Bill Borcherdt, ACSW, BCD
**Board Certified Diplomate
in Clinical Social Work**

**Professional Resource Press
Sarasota, Florida**

Published by Professional Resource Press
(An imprint of Professional Resource Exchange, Inc.)
Post Office Box 15560
Sarasota, FL 34277-1560

Copyright © 1996 by Professional Resource Exchange, Inc.

All rights reserved

Printed in the United States of America

With the limited exception noted below, no part of this book may be reproduced, stored in a retrieval system, or transmitted, in any form or by any means, either electronic, mechanical, photocopying, microfilming, recording, or otherwise, without written permission from the publisher. The guides in this book may be reproduced by purchasers solely for use with their clients in therapeutic settings. Any reproduction for any other purpose, including but not limited to resale or other distribution, without prior written permission from the publisher is prohibited and may be regarded as unlawful usage of copyrighted materials.

The copy editor for this book was Patricia Rockwood, the managing editor was Debra Fink, the production coordinator was Laurie Girsch, and the cover was created by Carol Tornatore.

Library of Congress Cataloging-in-Publication Data

Borcherdt, Bill.
      Head over heart in love : 25 guides to rational passion / Bill Borcherdt.
         p.   cm.
      Includes bibliographical references.
      ISBN 1-56887-017-5 (pbk. : alk. paper)
      1. Man-woman relationships. 2. Marriage--Psychological aspects.
      3. Rational-emotive psychotherapy. I. Title.
      HQ801.B765 1996
      306.7--dc20   95-53944
                                                                  CIP

Dedication

To Sharon for the abundance of love and loyalty that she has freely given.

To my parents, Zip and Lena, who, though long gone, are long remembered as two rare birds with an unusual talent for being themselves.

To my boyhood next-door neighbors, Marian and Floyd, who never relinquished the honeymoon stage, with admiration and appreciation for daily modeling the kind of joyful love life that I decided I wanted.

To Albert Ellis, a man of love and peace whose rational ideas have contributed to harmony the world over - and hopefully one day to world harmony.

Other books by Bill Borcherdt
Available from
Professional Resource Press
P.O. Box 15560
Sarasota, FL 34277-1560

Think Straight! Feel Great!
21 Guides to Emotional Self-Control

You Can Control Your Feelings!
24 Guides to Emotional Well-Being

Publisher's Note

This publication is designed to provide accurate and authoritative information in regard to the subject matter covered. It is sold with the understanding that the publisher is not engaged in rendering psychological, medical, or other professional services. If expert assistance or counseling is needed, the services of a competent professional should be sought.

Table of Contents

Introduction

Much of what I know about helping couples improve their relationships was learned as a student of Dr. Albert Ellis. His wisdom and my subsequent elaboration on his teachings form the basis for what I will teach you in this book.

Rational Emotive Behavior Therapy (REBT), as created by Dr. Ellis, takes a noncommercialized, unconventional yet civilized, humanistic approach to love relationships. A majority of people who seek professional counseling have love relationship problems. I would estimate that 80% to 90% of clients whom I have seen in psychotherapy over the past 29 years have had bonding difficulties. Such love concerns are not always expressed as the presenting problem, but as I get to know clients, usually in the first session, it becomes quite apparent that love life stresses and strains are a significant part of their problem picture. I think that my clients' high percentage of love difficulties are about the same as the prevalence of these problems in the general population. When it comes to gaining and sustaining a love relationship, couples often find themselves hamstrung! Enter REBT.

Dr. Ellis is a genius in the field of understanding and treating emotional and relationship problems and disturbances. One of the most profound thinkers of our time, his originality was not initially understood or appreciated. In time, Dr. Ellis's persistence paid off, and many of the therapists who originally scoffed when he presented his creative ideas now acclaim him as perhaps the all-time most influential figure in the study and practice of the art and science of psychotherapy. Dr. Ellis's *Institute for Rational-Emotive Therapy* is the central focal point for teaching REBT techniques. There are now nationally and internationally based Rational Emotive Behavior Therapy Centers and REBT's cognitive, emotive, and behavioral ideas are practiced by thousands of therapists all over the globe, a good number of whom were trained by Dr. Ellis and his Institute staff. Readers interested in receiving the Institute's semi-annual brochure describing its various educational and training seminars and psychoeducational materials (e.g., books, pamphlets, posters, audio- and videotapes, etc.) can request one by writing the Institute at 45 East 65th Street, New York, NY 10021.

Dr. Ellis began his professional career as a marriage and family counselor. It seems only natural that his vast influence on the field of human behavior has been especially focused on the challenges and joys of navigating love relationships.

Contrary to conventional wisdom, REBT tries to teach couples that as significant as love may seem to them, they need not be its victims. As important as love connections are, they are not all-important or sacred. It is this nonessential, healthier perspective on love attachments that allows couples to approach their goals in a more clear-headed and rational fashion. Learning nondesperate means of trying to "strike it rich" in living and learning how to develop a rich, juicy love life has distinct advantages over lives directed by more demanding, forced, love as "life or death" philosophies.

Some of the distinctive rational ideas that set REBT apart from other love-building or problem-solving methods will now be identified. The first three ideas (in the list below) are especially significant because they highlight issues that are ignored by other theories and therapies. Failure to understand these distinctions can result in the solution becoming the problem; the cure, the disease. REBT avoids these entrapments and consequently its ideas, when studied and practiced, typically result in feelings of self-control, contentment, and satisfaction with the evidence of improved relationships.

1. REBT helps people understand that they may strongly want, wish for, desire, and prefer love without trapping themselves into believing that they must have love or that they have an absolute need for love. REBT goes against the grain of commercialized suggestions that "love is what you need." Being cared for tenderly by another human is one of the most comforting experiences in the human condition. Yet, the split second this strong *preference* is made into a *necessity* is the moment individuals tighten themselves up emotionally, poisoning their most well-intended love-seeking efforts. REBT openly attacks this popular "need for love" fallacy, disproves it, and substitutes more flexible ideas that permit lovers to approach their relationships in a more relaxed, joyful, and emotionally stable manner.

2. REBT pinpoints the distinction between judging traits and outcomes and judging people. REBT avoids the rating game whereby individuals judge themselves by their love life performances and outcomes. When you or your partner act badly, neither of you is bad! If you fail in your love life, you are not a failure! This acceptance of yourself and others is a great relief. Knowing that you don't have to judge yourself or your partner by the outcome of your relationship relieves a great deal of pressure. It permits a more informal, light-hearted approach to your strivings for love.

3. REBT teaches people to more thoroughly get rid of their upsets rather than just expressing their upsetting feelings. Some therapies encourage couples to endlessly express their anger, hurt, and self-pity: REBT therapists view these techniques as destructive since they increase the very emotional disturbances people wish to eliminate. As mates react and overreact, they make themselves more emotionally disturbed and greatly handicap their hopes for a successful love life. This is because when you practice whining and complaining, you only learn to become a better whiner. REBT teaches people to dis-

solve their upsets *without* either openly expressing their negative emotions *or* ignoring them. REBT is a win-win approach to resolving personal and relationship problems.

4. REBT makes clear that flawed relationship interactions do not disturb people! Instead, people disturb themselves with their irrational thoughts and emotions about faulty interactions. REBT promotes the idea that love relationship problems can best be remedied by addressing the dysfunctional thoughts and emotions of partners. As individuals learn how to minimize their own emotional upset, they will be better able to use their increased tolerance and creativity to improve their relationship.

5. REBT consistently seeks philosophical solutions as the preferable problem-solving method. Teaching people how to change behavior patterns (e.g., through communication training and other types of relationship skill-building methods) is an important part of REBT's approach to improving love relationships. However, such practical procedures are not likely to be helpful until *after* couples have learned to minimize their emotional disturbances. In other words, couples will have much difficulty learning more effective communication skills if they are too emotionally upset to use these skills.

6. REBT highlights the value of not simply trying to "patch up" and "make things right" with couples. Instead, it more thoroughly and comprehensively teaches principles of emotional self-control that will allow couples to get themselves less upset when things go wrong in their relationship.

7. REBT looks at the assumptions and inferences that couples make about each other's actions and staunchly maintains that it is the irrational beliefs about these assumptions that creates disturbances in relationships. For instance, one partner may infer that his or her mate purposefully and intentionally calculated a plan to emotionally harm the partner. Such an inference, whether right

or wrong, creates some degree of irritation or displeasure. However, the demanding belief that the other person "must not" or "has no right" to purposefully discriminate in these ways results in emotional disturbances such as anger, rage, and fury.

8. REBT strongly emphasizes disputing and arguing against irrational love beliefs. In other words, each partner is encouraged to question the rationality of their beliefs and to reframe those beliefs in ways that will be less emotionally upsetting, prior to trying to change a couple's ways of relating to one another. The reader is referred to the Appendix on pages 145-166 which reprints a chapter from one of my previous books, *You Can Control Your Feelings!* (Borcherdt, 1993). The chapter is entitled, "I've Got the Fever, But Do You Really Have the Cure? Love Dependency: Complexities, Complications, and Corrections." This chapter reviews 26 irrational beliefs about love and how they can be rationally disputed.

9. REBT defines all rejection as self-rejection. If you enter into a love relationship with the understanding that no one can put you down but you, you won't worry about being rejected. More of love's potential can be better released in such a nonthreatening environment.

10. REBT delineates the important distinction between (a) putting your loved one first and yourself a distant second, and (b) putting yourself first and your partner a close second. Putting yourself first will minimize the resentments that frequently emerge in love relationships.

11. REBT stresses using your love life to improve your own mental health. The more you learn to deal with differences of opinion and relationship frustrations by increasing your tolerance, acceptance, and forgiveness levels, the better your chances of bringing more quality and contentment into all aspects of your life.

12. REBT distinguishes between normal and healthy love relationships. I recently counseled a couple in the aftermath of an extramarital affair between the husband and

a female work associate. The appointment was made at the request of the wife, who stated that her purpose in doing so was to get a decision from her husband as to whether he wanted to remain married to her or to continue his life with the other woman. Furthermore, she indicated that if he did choose to remain with the other woman, she would wish them happiness together. She mainly wanted to be clear on whom he would choose to cast his lot with, but she was not demanding that it be her. Her response to and her request about the affair were not normal, but they certainly were healthy. She didn't depress or anger herself, and she didn't take on a furor of hate and despisement as a huge majority in her situation would have. Instead, she took on a civilized outlook and began to conduct herself accordingly. Normal responses are those that the majority of people will have to a given life circumstance, not necessarily those that are healthy and helpful.

Some years ago another female client discovered her husband in bed with another woman. Rather than respond in the expected, conventional way of threatening to kill him, herself, or both, she more rationally decided, "If that is what he wants, that is his choice - so be it." Being able to exercise such civilized options in difficult times is a rare occurrence. Very few people will choose a nondemanding option in their love life. Instead, they usually enter into a love relationship with the notion that "I'll bond with you, I'll attach to you, I'll connect if not fuse with you, with the understanding that you must give me a return on my investment - and if you don't I'll hate, despise, and resent you until the day you die - and I hope it's soon!" In short, rational love is a nondemanding endeavor that is made to happen infrequently. A rational philosophy states, "I'll attach, bond, and connect with you and I will hope that you attach back to me as I would like, but there is no evidence that you must give me a return on my investment. I will continue to want a return from you but will not insist that you provide me with what I strongly desire." A small minority of love's participants will engage in such a rational view, but we can learn from those mavericks, who will likely experience a more pleasant, relaxed, and more joyful love life.

13. REBT strongly discourages black-or-white, all-or-nothing, absolutist thinking. REBT addresses and minimizes the three core irrational beliefs that create practically all relationship emotional upsets:

- "I have to be the perfect lover and mate or else I'm perfectly worthless." This belief creates guilt and shame because you inevitably will not be able to reach this perfectionistic goal.
- "You have to treat me forever lovingly or else you are perfectly worthless." This demand will result in a bad case of anger, vindictiveness, resentment, rage, and fury. This belief blocks kinder and gentler relationship possibilities.
- "The people around me have to make it easy for me to feel loved and happy." This ultra-insistence on others to treat you well will cause self-pity and lethargy when you inevitably discover that the world refuses to devote itself to your personal happiness.

14. REBT is more than a set of procedures and tactics to help you control for what you want so you can *feel* better. Rather, it persuasively assists you to *get* better by teaching you a method of thinking that transcends whether you succeed or fail to accomplish your goals. REBT advocates the "ABCDE model" for gaining self-control and better insuring your own happiness. For example, at point "A" (adversity, activating event) you may discover that although you would like your mate to agree with you on an important matter, you realize that he or she not only disagrees with you, but harshly criticizes you for your position on the matter (e.g., "I think your idea is

stupid and you're a fool for having it"). How you feel at point "C" (feelings, emotional consequences) about this cold prickly comment by one you love will mainly be determined by what you think to yourself at point "B" (belief system, thoughts, ideas) about what "A" means for you. If you have told yourself dysfunctional, distressing thoughts about your partner's comments (e.g., "She has no right to be so harsh with me, I would never address her in such pointed ways . . . How absolutely horrible it is to be required to listen to such hostile chatter . . . I cannot bear having him make mincemeat out of me . . . He is an absolute poor excuse for a human being for acting in these rotten ways and toward me of all people, the one who loves him"), you can move on to "D" (different ways of thinking, dispute, debate). At "D," you begin to talk more sense to yourself (e.g., "Due to my loved one's free will and human limitations, she has a right to act badly toward me . . . why do I have to make it out to be so gruesome just because I have been exposed to his hostile mumblings? . . . Her comments are certainly not pleasant, yet she did not harm me . . . As badly as my mate acts, he is not a bad person." This more tolerant, accepting way of thinking will take you to "E" (new thoughts and feelings) where you will think, feel, and act differently, and respond more constructively to your mate (e.g., you will still express to yourself a distinct preference for being better understood by your partner, feel disappointed or annoyed by his or her comments, and have the freedom to tell your partner directly that you dislike his or her conduct, but you will not unduly disturb yourself by overreacting to and "taking personally" your mate's criticisms in ways that damage you and your relationship). Many of the traits we dislike in those we love the most won't change a great deal. The trick is to not disturb ourself when our little heart's desires are not met. It is from this position of increased grace, tolerance, and forgiveness that we stand in a better position to influence events in our relationships with those we love.

In the chapters that follow, I will present specific suggestions to you and your partner on ways to increase your contentment with yourself and your mate and improve the joyful aspects of your relationship.

Love has potential to grow. However, until we learn to unblock ourselves by curtailing emotional upsets about what we don't adore in our partners, we will be less able to create growth and improvements. By training ourselves to limit our emotional upsets, we can put more enjoyment, excitement, and exhilaration into our lives. "Grin and bear it" can be replaced with "grin and enjoy it." *Wreck*reation can be replaced with *re*creation. The myth of living *happily* ever after can be substituted with the reality of living *happier* ever after. By applying the various methods of thought, feelings, and behaviors described in this book to your relationships with those you love, you can experience the true joys of rational loving and living.

Bill Borcherdt, ACSW
January, 1996

HEAD OVER HEART IN LOVE:
25 GUIDES TO RATIONAL PASSION

A Couple Who
Laughs Together,
Stays Together

- A couple with whom I recently counseled began to vividly describe one of their fights. The woman explained how she had thrown a hot cup of coffee at her mate. I racked my brain, and the only thing I could think of in response to her portrayal was, "Was it caf or de-caf?"
- A woman was ranting and raving, angrily describing her mate's negative traits. In the middle of her seeming unceasing emotional tirade she abruptly stopped herself, moved to the edge of her chair, glared at me, and stated, "I'll bet you think that I would be a bitch to live with." After a moment's hesitation I responded, "No, I'd shape you up."
- After a long-winded session with a couple who were very much at odds with one another, the man asked, "Should we shake hands?" "No," I responded, "You might come out fighting."
- While out for a jog on a Sunday morning, a couple with whom I had been counseling drove up to me in their car and stopped. "Guess what?" the man asked. "Now what?" I replied. "We haven't fought yet today," he stated. "Yes," I said, "But the day is still young."
- A couple entered my office in a particularly sour, grumpy mood. I asked them a standard opening question: "How can I help you?" The female firmly responded, "Well, we

certainly don't expect miracles!" To which I countered, "Well, I'm certainly sorry, but I'm going to have to disappoint you!"

After the punch line in each of these five instances, the participants snickered, smiled, and laughed. A good, honest beginning avenue for problem solving was then established, because humorous interactions can lead the way toward constructive relationship problem solving. Without the emotional lift that results from humor, problem solving and the joys that can follow are likely to get lost in a sea of bickering. These illustrations also show how humor can be found even in situations that are not funny - such as throwing a hot cup of coffee at someone.

Laughing together will likely help keep couples together - provided they laugh *with* each other more than *at* each other. An intertwining sense of humor can be used to support the "we" and "us" factors in a love relationship. Laughter brings people together and keeps them together. It invites you to be more attracted to and results in you being more attractive for your loved one. It can help you get over the humps and hurdles of, as well as turn the corners in, your love relationships. It relieves some of the stress from all the things that don't add up in your attempts to better understand the "you, me, and us" in your relationship. Love without laughter is like a car without shocks, jarred by each dip in the road. Without laughter, love relationships are made into an experience of "all work and no play" - making for a "dull boy and girl." Laughter sprinkles love with fun, making its seeming mountains appear more like the molehills that they often are.

This chapter will first identify some cautions in using humor in love relationships and then list the advantages of humor in paving the way for promoting acceptance of individual differences. First, what to avoid in the expression of humor:

1. *Encouraging shame or embarrassment.* Honestly examine your motives. If you find that your intention is to "do

another in" emotionally rather than subsidize his or her emotional well-being, put that jest on the back burner.

2. *Excessiveness.* Too much of a good thing is made into bad. Humor is not the answer to everything and therefore not appropriate every time, in every situation. If not regulated, helpful humor can be turned into immature giddiness, where life and love are turned into one big tease.

3. *Gallows humor.* Crusty comments such as, "You look handsome in that new outfit - especially since you're 30 pounds heavier than the day we got married" or "Dear, you look gorgeous - today," can lead to a hardening of feelings toward one another.

4. *Ego heavens and ego hells.* Seemingly humorous comments that are really forms of psychological "one-up" and "one-down" are best ruled out. Cracks that hit on a skill or positive feature that you have, while making fun of someone else who doesn't possess such advantages, are a dead giveaway that you are humorously trying to prove your absolute superiority over another.

5. *Sarcastic, caustic comments that are directed toward the jugular vein of another's sensitivities.* Hitting below the belt at your mate's vulnerabilities, however bleached in humor your comments may be, leaves you laughing *at* rather than *with* your partner. Find better, softer manners of humor as communication lest you contribute to a hardening of feelings.

6. *Ask yourself if you want to install bridges or build walls.* Do some consequential thinking. Look at the track record of your humor methods. Do they bring you closer or contribute to being further apart? Are they supportive or destructive of your long-range relationship goals? Do they affirm or question another's strengths? Is your playfulness a validating expression of your love or a childish expression of dominance?

7. *Distinguish claim from disclaim.* Gauge impact. Do your humor expressions really do what you claim they do by way of lighting up and highlighting your love life or do

they disclaim your bonding ideals? This final spot check suggests that you reexamine your motives, manners, and methods one last time to better assure that they are in sync with love's long-range happiness and survival.

Let's assume you are able to get yourself past the preceding pitfalls. What advantages does well-intended humor provide when backed up by the right methods?

1. *Counters demandingness.* Love attachment makes the world go around, but demands for a return attachment will make you dizzy. Couples who don't take themselves so seriously that they can't laugh together will likely be less demanding of one another and consequently will be more inclined to stay together.
2. *Prevents emotional confusion/dizziness.* Humor provides relief for the stresses and strains that are a part of resolving ever-present individual differences.
3. *Increases tolerance.* Tolerance won't make for a happy love life, but it is unlikely you will have a happier love life without it. Dr. Albert Ellis, founder of Rational Emotive Behavior Therapy, points out that when you laugh at yourself you increase your tolerance levels. Not taking yourself too seriously in this way will facilitate this same tolerance in relating to others.
4. *Feeds into a philosophy of happiness and joy.* Humor is an expression of joy; as such, it often results in behavioral jubilation.
5. *Becomes one of the ultimate expressions of love.* Perhaps the most loving thing you can do for people is to not take them as seriously as they are taking themselves.
6. *Means less caution and more freewheelingness.* Barriers of hesitation are overcome when you replace tightening up with lightening up.
7. *Leads to less defensiveness and guardedness.* Overexplaining and tip-toeing around disagreements are discouraged when such issues are not taken dead seriously. As a result, important issues can see the light and enlightenment of day.

8. *Discourages self-proving conduct.* Those who have the wherewithal to laugh at themselves are less inclined to try to prove themselves to one another.

9. *Combats fear.* Fear of relationship failure will make you more inclined to bring on loss. Laughter facilitates the kind of emotional balance that makes for a steadier hand on the relationship throttle.

10. *Exposes personality flaws and shortcomings in a nonthreatening way.* As such, humor results in a more well-rounded personality.

11. *Has some democratic, equalization qualities.* Finding humor in your deficiencies gives off the message, "No pretenses please, we're both in this together and neither is better than the other."

12. *Energizes and involves.* Anticipation and participation is often ignited from humor's sparks.

13. *Signals hope.* Laughter at yourself and your problems sends the message that you tend to prevail over any or all hard times there are or could befall you.

14. *Becomes a mechanism of self- and other discovery.* Laughter can reveal character. Humor lowers your guard while exposing thoughts, feelings, and behaviors that you may have never known existed in you and yours.

15. *Provides a standard for and an island of reality.* Humor provides a unique method for identifying reality, which can often be too funny to be taken seriously. It can also set you apart from the maddening crowd and in this way provide a healthful, unconventional respite from conventional toil.

16. *Contributes to harmony and goodwill.* Increased camaraderie and delight in the relationship springs from looking at life and love from the lighter side.

17. *Maintains attention and retention.* Laughter can bring attention to important life areas and then help to retain that information by the humorous, novel illustrations associated with them.

18. *Helps to expect the unexpected while increasing concentration in doing so.* Laughter gets the cobwebs out when puzzled

about what to make out of unexpected events in the relationship.

19. *Unleashes creativity.* Giving yourself some humorous emotional slack can result in discovering unique ways of looking at relationship circumstances.

20. *Influences, invites others to be more favorably disposed toward you.* Humor lubricates relationships in a way that makes you hard to resist. Most people are looking for a good laugh. By accommodating their funny bone you convenience their gravitating more toward you while giving fuller consideration to your opinions.

21. *Encourages relationship experimentation.* Because humor has a flair to it, its expressions have a loosening-up effect that can prompt testing and tasting of new, potentially enriching things to do together.

22. *Encourages alertness, discourages take-for-grantedness.* Humor puts one on alert. As a result, relationship upkeep is likely to be more consistent.

23. *Reinforces the idea that you are likely to get more bees with honey than with vinegar.* Humor as a positive expression appreciates that relationships are better built by focusing on others' strengths rather than on their weaknesses and by appreciating rather than depreciating them.

24. *Builds cooperation and compromise.* Humor neutralizes anger and resentment; as a result, helpful collaboration will more often prevail.

25. *Demonstrates that you understand another in an unusual way, to an unusual degree.* Humor can be a unique in-depth expression by way of the understanding that is communicated in and lies behind the laughter.

26. *Expresses a vote of confidence.* Being humorous with someone implies, "I don't think you're a sourpuss that I must walk on thin ice around; I think you can take it."

27. *Deflects and defeats potentially awkward moments.* Strokes of humor are often just the tonic to buffer unsure moments.

28. *Is hard to refute.* It is difficult to argue with people who present themselves in a humorous manner.

29. *Separates your faults from yourself.* Humor allows you to take your faults seriously but yourself lightly.
30. *Conveys self-acceptance and self-confidence.* The notion that "I undamningly accept myself in spite of my imperfections" lies at the base of laughing at yourself.

Note. From *Head Over Heart in Love: 25 Guides to Rational Passion* by Bill Borcherdt. Copyright © 1996, Professional Resource Exchange, Inc., P.O. Box 15560, Sarasota, FL 34277-1560.

Two Wrongs Don't Make a Right: Righting Love By Not Duplicating Wrong

A couple whom I recently counseled reflected on the negative state of their marriage and wondered how things were made to go so wrong - and what could be done to make them go right. What they discovered was 20 years of neglect of domestic matters by the husband and 20 years of neglect of self-interest by the wife. He by overdoing his job duties and underdoing his domestic responsibilities; she overdoing by trying to be all things to all people at home, wearing her fingers to the bone for others and in the process giving herself bony fingers! Love and compatibility eroded, with each wondering whether the only thing they had in common was the fact that they had been married on the same day! Each in their own way had contributed to the teetering of their relationship: he more by what he didn't do, she more by what she in vain tried too hard to do.

This is a common pattern. The result is often the same: partners fall out of love, though the "two wrongs don't make a right" mechanism for doing so may be different. This chapter will identify and explain variations of a common theme of two partners going down different blind alleys, confused as to why they aren't able to find their way home to a more pleasant, compatible relationship. Remedies for avoiding this syndrome will be offered. Examples of duplicating another's error in an opposite, sometimes oppositional manner include:

1. The common imbalance illustrated earlier where one partner, usually the man, buries his head in the sand and overlooks his lack of participation in home-centered activities. At the same time, his mate sweeps under the rug any personal ambitions that she has, ending up not only sharing her life with her family but unwisely sacrificing her life for them.

2. An overreactive-underreactive pattern is established when partner number one foolishly angers himself or herself when not getting his or her own way. Partner number two then purposely clams up, choosing to sulk about rather than try to address the matter of concern. These opposing communication styles are poor problem-solving, anticollaborative methods that block the possibilities for compromise.

3. When an overreactive-overreactive communication stance is established, couples put themselves in an imitative pattern. This occurs when one mate angers himself or herself about the other's anger; this sequence results in emotional disturbance being mass-produced, as both partners do battle under the code of "an eye for an eye, and a tooth for a tooth" - which results in a lot of blind, toothless people walking around.

4. Relationships where one mate tries to do the communication work of two people become a breeding ground for emotional dependency and mutual resentment. If one partner finds that efforts to get the mate to "open up" are like pulling teeth, yet continues to attempt to coax him or her into being more inclined to spill the verbal beans, the dependency of the communicator to engage the other is reinforced with the noncommunicator resenting what is interpreted as nagging.

5. To err is human; to blame is even more human. Mutually blaming one another for what goes wrong is another

human tendency that will pile one misery on another. Retaliation - fighting blaming fire with more blaming fire - only heaps additional emotional upset on a fire that has already gotten out of hand.

6. Consistently accepting blame when not at fault can also be made into a pot of resentment. Too quickly taking responsibility for something that went wrong when you did no wrong frequently leads the way to unangry restraint fast on the heels of angry restraint.

7. Bending over backwards to excessively please others who are difficult to please may temporarily pacify them while neutralizing whatever power you think the other might have over you. However, such strenuous efforts to be ingratiating often backfire by conveniencing resentment due to your futile efforts to please someone who refuses to be pleased. Both the easily annoyed and the placator lose in this faulty relationship arrangement.

8. An ultra-conservative, nonrisk-taking-to-a-fault partner who is countered by a risk-taking-to-the-point-of-being-foolhardy mate are both asking for trouble. A wrong-doer is not only someone who has done something wrong (in the case of the overly permissive mate) but also someone who does virtually nothing by way of approaching life in a more adventuresome, risk-taking way. Two extremes block the harmony that may be someplace in between.

9. Overcontrolling people who think they are required - if not anointed - to be the final authority in decision making can usually have their own way when matched with an excessively compliant partner. In the short run such one-sidedness would seem to be harmless, but in the long run compliance is often a prelude to complaining. Two wrongful extreme methods of decision making make it difficult to attain a right relationship balance.

10. When you and your partner echo each other's expression of exaggeration and low frustration tolerance, this contributes to a relationship climate that reeks with stress

and strain. Evaluative judgments about life circumstances such as "I can't stand it" or "It's terrible, awful, and horrible" that are preceded by your partner's similar anguishing notions is yet another example of how two excessives do not make a happier medium.

11. True-believer tendencies that have both mates staunchly standing up for their values with a fearful determination to not back down often results in a fight-or-flight response. The favorite opposing means of dealing with these brands of dogged, yet wrongful determination are often either openly feuding or avoiding controversy at all costs.

Suggestions for righting love by not duplicating wrong are:

1. *Draw a line in the sand sooner, not later.* The best time to correct a bad habit is as soon as you notice its existence. If you sense that you are doing too many things for others that they would be better off doing for themselves, clearly identify the point at which you will stop helping others.

2. *Think ahead and prepare.* Expect to encounter opportunities to take bad opposing situations and make them worse. Then, mentally prepare yourself to pass on those duplicating wrong temptations.

3. *Admit to your gullible, suggestible, imitative tendencies.* Then, don't put yourself down for having them but make a plan to decisively change your way of thinking from "If my mate can act badly, so can I" to "Because my mate acts badly that doesn't mean that I can't think for myself and decide to take independent, more constructive action."

4. *Make part of your relationship philosophy the idea that when your mate treats you unfairly this is all the more reason to be fair to yourself - by not making yourself miserable by blowing a bad disagreement out of proportion.*

5. *Don't exaggerate, yet don't "keep a stiff upper lip" to a fault.* Don't treat molehills of concern as if they were moun-

tains, but don't tolerate another's neglect or disturbances indefinitely. Make an educated guess on when it might be time to raise the consciousness of the relationship so as to not be overrun by it.

6. *Promote rotation and balance.* Counter one-sidedness by suggesting more give-and-take regarding who does what around the house and with each other (e.g., rotate who suggests weekend activities).

7. *Exchange wish lists - and honor them.* Write out those aspects of your relationship that you think are out of kilter and wish to be changed. Then, take a gander at your partner's so as to begin relationship fine-tuning.

8. *Set aside time for a listening exercise that encourages you to assess your relationship as you both go along.* Rather than wait for problems to stockpile, get them out on the table. One method of doing this would be to apply the following 10-minute communication exercise. Set aside the time to do the following once or twice a week:

   - One partner goes first and talks for precisely 2 minutes about something that is important for him or her.
   - The listener then gives the talker feedback about the content that was heard and more importantly the feelings sensed about the content; for example, "I heard you say . . . and it sounds like you felt . . . about what you said."
   - The talker gives the listener feedback about the listener's feedback; for example, "You're right, I did say . . . and I did feel . . . about. . . ."
   - The same three steps are followed as the talker becomes the listener.

9. *Identify individual responsibilities.* This is a simple but not an easy thing to do. Don't let yourself get caught in your own insecure defensiveness. Boldly state what contributions you are presently making to the difficulties in the relationship and what you can *and will* do to contribute to relationship improvement.

10. *Notice others' as well as your own efforts.* Inspire hope while understanding that good behavior gone unnoticed is less likely to occur.
11. *Rekindle the "good old days" and what you were doing right way back when, so as not to double up on your differences.*
12. *Vow to do things differently and to do different things.* Create sources of new interests in your relationship that will take your mind off and you away from relationship-hindering, business-as-usual handicaps.
13. *Collaborate as a partnership against common poisons of relationship building such as overreaction, stagnation, suggestibility, and procrastination.* Develop an attitude of us against the human condition - where we run it rather than it runs us. Accept the fact that you're not going to be perfect or form the perfect team, that you're going to lose some battles but yet still win the war against relationship do-nothingism or overdoingism.
14. *Use restraining self-talk such as:*

 * "Best I rock the boat now so I don't drown later."
 * "Level in a levelheaded way."
 * "Fighting fire with fire will only get me burned."
 * "Better that I not try too hard to do the relationship work of two people."
 * "Blaming bruises."
 * "Set limits by drawing a line in the sand rather than burying your head in it."
 * "If I keep bending over backwards without saying anything in the short run, I will likely break the back of our relationship in the long run."
 * "Pay less now, or more later; short-run sacrifices of discomfort lead to more comfort later on."
 * "Do I want to feel better now by continuing to go along with the gag or do I want to feel better for the rest of my life by taking a stand?"
 * "Make your own decisions - you're the one who lives with them."

- "Be concerned but not consumed."
- "Proving myself will likely get me nowhere fast; being myself gives me more options."

"Often imitated, never duplicated" is often experienced as "too often imitated and practically always duplicated" when it comes to strife in love relationships. Make it a point to not take the togetherness-disruption ball and run with it, and you'll discover the key to long-range relationship success. Make sure your right hand knows what your left hand is doing in your efforts toward righting love, lest you cause yourself to be left out in the cold war of conflict rather than better accommodating the real world of individual differences.

Note. From *Head Over Heart in Love: 25 Guides to Rational Passion* by Bill Borcherdt. Copyright © 1996, Professional Resource Exchange, Inc., P.O. Box 15560, Sarasota, FL 34277-1560.

Circle the Wagons:
Substituting You and Me
Against Each Other for
You and Me Against the World

No relationship is ideal. Sustaining a good love life requires all the help two people can muster. One way of gaining the edge in favor of love rather than living on the edge of love's hopes is to identify and cultivate a common enemy. Don't beat it to death, mind you, but this other-directed love-improvement strategy can provide a unique advantage for your relationship. Examples of how negative common ground can contribute to a more positive relationship include: a common cause such as supporting an environmental project; actively campaigning for a political party; plotting to protect yourselves against the wiles of a difficult-acting relative; or writing a joint letter to the editor that reflects your strong concerns about a controversial community happening. An unusual bonding can be made to happen by such active expressions of common grievances.

Coming together in this focused way can provide many advantages in the service of developing a higher quality relationship. Here is a sampling of them:

1. *Deflects emotions.* Upset normally reserved for one another can be rerouted to a third party. Hence, emotional wear and tear is avoided.

2. *Establishes a common passion and emotional revitalization.*
   The joint force of such intensity of emotion can rekindle
   emotional strength. Such emotional reawakenings can
   be directed toward the benefit of your relationship.
3. *Distracts from individual differences.* Disagreements left
   unattended while expressing disenchantment toward an
   outside offender lessens conflicts and, in this indirect way,
   puts a more positive bead on your relationship.
4. *Reinforces a "united we stand," "we're in this together" philosophy.* Strength in togetherness ideals has been known
   to help keep lovers together.
5. *Can bring to light the facts of common interests otherwise gone
   unnoticed.* Identifying a common enemy can jog your
   mind as to what other vital absorptions you may have in
   common.
6. *Provides a qualitative basis for comparison.* By zeroing in on
   common enemies, you may discover that any dislike for
   your mate's negative traits is a drop in the bucket when
   contrasted with your despisement for your opponents.
   This realization can help you to better appreciate what
   advantages you have in being with your mate.
7. *Allows you to practice planning, scheming, and structuring
   your time for a common goal.* Learning how to confer with
   your partner in creating a road map to accomplish the
   common goal of defeating a common enemy requires
   skills that can be put to use in future projects. Each such
   outing can help strengthen your attachment to one another while increasing your problem-solving skills.
8. *Provides relationship success confidence.* Confidence in your
   joint problem-solving abilities is established with each
   accomplishment of fending off a common enemy.
9. *Generally improves communication.* The give-and-take of
   heated conversations about a theme or a negative-acting
   person can arouse conversational capacities about many
   things in life.
10. *Helps to avoid beating your own differences - and love life - to
    death.* Distraction and diversionary benefits are gained

when scrutinizing a third party's faults. Such methods of transferring complaints will take pressure off your love life.

11. *Can teach you how not to do it.* Highlighting an outsider's faults can serve as a reminder not to behave in the same negative fashion yourself.
12. *Allows compromises to be more easily practiced.* Compromising opinions about someone else's problems and disturbances are easier to arrive at than those closer to home. Getting a taste of successful conflict resolution about differing opinions of others can lead to more agreement about your own relationship differences.
13. *Provides a respite.* A time-out from your own differences while bird-dogging your dislikes for others' negative traits may be a good opportunity to gather your thoughts and reassess your views of your own faults.

What are some guidelines to follow in forming an alliance against a negative-acting intruder? Here are four steps to consider:

1. Directly make yourselves aware that such united possibilities exist; for instance: "What do you think of the two of us banding together against _____ to see if we can influence/change him/her/it?" "I think _____ is going too far, what do you think about us putting our heads together and see if we can't do something about it?" "I think we have been trying way too hard to change one another. What do you think of the idea of us brainstorming ways we can channel that energy in the direction of someone/something that we don't approve of?"
2. Once mutual consent is arrived at, gather suggestions that will begin a plan of action.
3. Initiate a plan, then reflect upon, appreciate, and fine-tune your efforts.

4. Repeat, so as to smooth out your tact and tactics.

While preparing for this common-enemy venture, use thoughts that will assist in successfully completing this plot:

GO FROM	TO
"I've got a bone to pick with you."	"Let's find bones to pick with someone else."
"I don't like the way you have been acting lately."	"I never did like the way he/she has acted."
"You bug me."	"I'm bugging myself about _____."
"I'll get even with you."	"Let's show him/her a thing or two."
"I can't stand being around you."	"I don't like being around him/her/that. Will you help me on the matter?"
"All we do is fight like the worst of enemies."	"Let's find someone else we can settle differences with."
"We never share anything together."	"Let's pull together to defeat _____."
"It's been along time since we have had shared feelings."	"I think we both have some strong feelings on this matter; what do you say we share them?"

Pooling your resources against a common enemy is one unique way of bolstering a love relationship. Yet, it is far from a complete cure for all that ails your love life, and it's best not used as a substitute for a more complete over-haul. Find its place in the overall scheme of your love-life-improvement methods. This form of symptom substitution doesn't come to terms with how you upset yourselves in relationship to one another, but it can at least temporarily create the camaraderie helpful for the purpose of backing up and starting over again in resolving your differences - with a fresher outlook. Interlocking your differences toward a third party may be one of those methods that will assist in unlocking secrets to a successful love life. Gather your forces and see!

Note. From *Head Over Heart in Love: 25 Guides to Rational Passion* by Bill Borcherdt. Copyright © 1996, Professional Resource Exchange, Inc., P.O. Box 15560, Sarasota, FL 34277-1560.

Don't Dish It Out Even If You *Can* Take It: Choosing Your Critical Words Carefully

Criticizing sparingly is a manner of showing respect for your partner's vulnerabilities. Such matters and manners of avoiding your loved one's sore spots contributes greatly to the quality of your love relationships. Porcupine teasing and thorny criticisms are not good methods for gaining and maintaining a pleasant togetherness. Perhaps the major downfall of love relationships is the two-sided coin of negative criticism - giving too much of it and taking it too seriously. Tapering if not restricting your crusty comments in certain areas is akin to not feeding your partner strawberries because he or she is physically allergic to them. Such off-limits decisions show respect for any emotional allergies your mate might give himself or herself, such as hurt or anger. With less emotional debris, such choices also provide a clearer field in which you can promote bigger and better relationship advantages.

Many people have difficulty taking criticism in stride. You may or may not be one of them. Don't assume that because something negative you might say or gesture toward another would be treated like "water off a duck's back" by you, that the other person isn't going to, "should," or "must" not squawk either. Humans are selective in what they overreact to. What is casual or appealing for one may be a casualty or appalling for another. There are very few who will let negative comment bounce off them as if they were the Rock of Gibraltar. It's a good idea to consider this human tendency toward selective hypersensitivity, and what those unique prickly topics are made out to be by your loved one, lest your relationship end up on the rocks.

The fact that you wouldn't offend yourself by your own wording is beside the point. Don't shoot from the hip and expect not to be fired back at. Walk a mile in the other's moccasins; take a weather reading; and get a sense for what the other's emotional temperature will likely be in the face of your verbal barrage. Then, exercise caution and discretion in determining whether or not to trip the trigger. Avoid such self-centered thinking as:

- "Well, I wouldn't mind being teased this way, so he shouldn't either."
- "She is just going to have to learn how to accept me and my manner of expression if she has any hopes of getting along with me."
- "Other people don't mind my manners, and there is no reason why he should either."
- "If she doesn't like it, that's her problem and she is going to have to solve it by herself."
- "I can dish it out as well as take it, and it's high time he learns to also."
- "Nobody has any justification for being so sensitive as she is. I'll just continue to criticize and tease until she gets used to it."
- "How dare he take me so seriously! I have never taken him so solemnly and therefore he should treat me with no lapses in toleration and lightheartedness."
- "What a killjoy! Here I am trying to be funny and she acts like such a serious-headed creep."
- "I thought relationships are supposed to be give-and-take. Well if I can give, why can't he take?"

- "I'm only being harsh with her for her own good. Why can't she tell that I'm only trying to help?"
- "That's gratitude for you. Here I am, working hard to improve his character for him and all I get in return is rebuff."

People who think this way don't appreciate that their loved ones are different from themselves. They also don't understand or accept that their ignorance and stupid refusal to choose their words more carefully are not only a problem for their partner, but may be even a bigger problem for themselves. Unless they change their negative-acting ways, they may strongly contribute to bringing a valued relationship to a screeching halt. Far better that they bend their contrary lingo by instead self-stating:

- "Better that I not foolishly presume that what I find sufficiently pleasant my loved one will too."
- "It would be wise of me to have a decent respect for individual differences in responding to the same words."
- "Because I have learned to not overreact to something doesn't mean others are required to take on the same learnings."
- "When people in my social group find what I say distasteful it is part my problem, especially if I regularly associate with them."
- "Perhaps if we are going to get along it might be more a case of me learning to accept and respect their sore spots than for them to accept my sore-headed statements."
- "Others can be as sensitive and solemn about what I say as their nature allows, and I would do well to gracefully accept their sensitivities rather than demand and command that they control them."
- "It would be a good idea to let others decide what's good for them by way of choosing their sensitivities. Who do I think I am anyway, their Fairy Godmother?"

- "It would be well for me to consider what someone else's rebuff of my comments speaks to and to slacken up, lest I convenience the other's turning against me."
- "My way of teasing may be appealing for some and appalling for others, and it is in my best interest to accept that one size doesn't fit all."
- "It's nice when relationships are built on the principle of give-and-take but *not* 50 I give and 50 they take."

Honoring another's sensitivities by avoiding them is a silent form of respect that is often quietly appreciated by the receiver. By realizing and accepting that others' reactions are not the same as your own, you can take an all-right relationship and make it better rather than contributing to it being made worse. Such a more careful choice of words allows you to dish out more nourishing portions of love that you can also more easily take.

Note. From *Head Over Heart in Love: 25 Guides to Rational Passion* by Bill Borcherdt. Copyright © 1996, Professional Resource Exchange, Inc., P.O. Box 15560, Sarasota, FL 34277-1560.

Insisting Upon Being Right:
Dying With the Right
Of False Pride On

Politicians from time to time say, "I'd rather be right than president." Partners in love more often than not apply the same principle in their relationship. By their insistences on being right, they are really communicating their preference for being right rather than staying in love. They may not intend to contribute to love's downfall by their demanding manner, but from a practical standpoint they are "throwing the baby out with the bathwater." Their self-command, "I have to be right" contributes to a spoiling effect on relationships; acting like a porcupine by this insistent approach discourages people from approaching them! Such compulsively driven activity is called false pride because it is a fearful attempt to disguise insecurity. This chapter will encourage ideas driven by personal happiness goals rather than ego-pride, self-proving ambitions. It will also review the tactics of addressing circumstances in which it is especially important to overcome the ego resistances that result in wrongly sticking to one's guns.

As difficult as it is to do certain things (e.g., adopt a philosophy of admittance), it is more difficult not to. After all, if you seldom, if ever, admit to your errors in the short run, you are unlikely to get around to correcting them in the long run. As a result, instead of furthering your personal and emotional development, you weaken if not kill it. It's difficult to get yourself beyond a point that you deny you haven't yet gotten to. Why the love affair with being right when it exists as a direct attack on and a threat to such an important area of life as love relationships? Below are some explanations for overemphasis on this self- and love-defeating behavior.

1. *Stubbornness, pigheadedness, bullheadedness, and block-headedness.* Different words with similar meanings of "digging in your heels," these descriptive terms reflect the peculiar sense of pride and smug satisfaction that goes along with refusing to consider being in the wrong.

2. *Concluding that being wrong is the same as being bad.* Identifying the blunder as a reflection of yourself encourages denial of wrongdoing.

3. *Assuming that being wrong is the same as being weak.* The self-confidence that prompts freely disclosing your mistakes is lost due to personal insecurities that result from a view that equates wrongness and failure with weakness.

4. *Low frustration tolerance.* Ideas similar to "I can't stand the discomforting humility that goes along with admitting that I, of all people, am wrong" prompt you to avoid putting yourself in such an emotional hot spot.

5. *Disapproval anxiety.* Fearing criticism from your social group will also prompt you to avoid coping with your mistakes at all costs.

6. *Guilt.* Believing that if you reveal faults that you would be required to put yourself down for having them puts a nonexposure philosophy into motion.

7. *Combats boredom and accommodates excitement-seeking tendencies.* Zealously, if not fanatically, clinging to your absolute rightness and another's certain wrongness often sparks boundary disputes that counter an otherwise ho-hum existence.

8. *Psychological one-up-personship strivings.* Believing that being right means being a better person encourages you to hang on to your conclusions for dear life.

9. *Mistaken, irrational ideas.* The ultimate explanation for human emotion and behavior is rooted in a person's philosophy of life. Humans come to their life circumstances with ideas about what each happening means for them. In the case of insisting on being right, such notions are grounded in:

- *Defensiveness* - "I am on trial and have to defend and overexplain myself against any and all possible wrong-doing."
- *Insecurity* - "I feel inferior to begin with; now, to admit my mistake on top of it all would be more exposure than my ego could handle."
- *Overreaction and Exaggeration* - "How absolutely and profoundly horrible it would be to admit that I am not right and to experience the excessive discomfort that would go along with such a revelation."
- *Overgeneralization* - "If I admit failure in being right I would be a failure as a human being."
- *Perfectionism* - "I must be perfectly right and leave others with no shadow of a doubt that this is the case."
- *Demandingness* - "I must be exactly right and you must supply me with such never-ending agreement that I am so."
- *Downingness* - "You and I are both jerks when wrong, so better you than me be classified as such. Therefore, I'm absolutely right and you're absolutely wrong - and don't you dare propose any other way of looking at it - you jerk!"
- *Grandiosity* - "I am a special person whose opinions are precious if not sacred and nobody, especially myself, can deny that."
- *Gullibility* - "I learned a long time ago that if you're in the wrong, you're the wrong kind of person. Better that I insistently define myself as being on the right side so that I can be the right kind of person."

These and other illogical ways of thinking can be challenged and corrected. In the following chart I will (a) give 10 examples of typical life circumstances where insisting on being right is made into an almighty option, (b) provide irrational ideas that result in increased relationship tension and emotional upset, and (c) illustrate logical views that can be substituted to better contribute to emotional and relationship well-being.

LIFE CIRCUMSTANCE	IRRATIONAL IDEA	LOGICAL SUBSTITUTING IDEA
1. Parenting	"His way of correcting the children is and always has been wrong."	"Neither I nor my mate has a monopoly on parenting expertise."
2. Money management	"I know my way of investing our money is the only way to go. I'll take care of the checkbook."	"There are many ways of investing money; my way is but one."
3. In-law contacts	"I know for sure that if we never visited our in-laws we would be a heap better off."	"Granted, I don't enjoy in-law visits. However, my mate does so, therefore I would do well to see visits to be not all bad."
4. Leisure/ vacation time	"I am the expert in the family regarding what to do with spare time; that's all there is to it."	"My mate may have thought of some interesting leisure activities that I didn't."
5. Employment/ vocational decisions	"I'll rightly decide who of the two of us is going to work outside of the home, when."	"This, like all our decisions, affects *both* of us; better that we both have input."
6. Household maintenance/ activities (e.g., cleaning, car repairs, laundry)	"She will help out with the upkeep that I decide she will do."	"Discussing rather than enforcing who will do what maintenance matters would be wise."

LIFE CIRCUMSTANCE	IRRATIONAL IDEA	LOGICAL SUBSTITUTING IDEA
7. Amount of time spent together/apart	"I know what's best for us and will decide how much space there will be between us."	"It's her life too. Better that *we* decide the you, me, and us time allotments."
8. Mutual friends	"I know whose personalities we have in common and therefore will rightly identify and be the one to strike up common relationships."	"My mate knows people too. Better that we encourage each other to share our knowledge."
9. Religious preference	"My religion is better than his and better for both of us."	"Let's see if I can find some value in each of our religions."
10. Hobbies and other pastimes	"If hobbies and other pastimes interfere with what I think is the right amount of quality time in our relationship, she will just have to give up at least some of them."	"Because her tastes are my poison doesn't mean that she is the only one who can bend."

The preceding practical tasks of extended love relationships can be made into a real hotbed of problems - especially when one or both mates jump up and down to prove the rightness of their case. It is such childish exhibitions that result in couples dying with their individual rights on. Supportive, affirmative, understanding statements heard from couples who determine not to perish their relationship include:

- "I'd like to hear some of your ideas on the matter."
- "I hear what you're saying."
- "There's a lot of truth in what you just said."
- "I'll bet you have some good thoughts on the topic."

- "Your ideas have been very helpful in the past; would you be willing to lend me some of your present thinking on the matter?"
- "It sounds like what you just said was well thought out."
- "I admire and appreciate the strength of your convictions."
- "I can practically always count on you to shed some light on these important matters."
- "Sounds like we both have strong opinions on the matter. What do you think of the idea of us putting our heads together and brainstorming a compromise?"
- "I can tell by how much thought that you have given this matter that our relationship means a lot to you."
- "How would you decide on something like this?"
- "I know myself well enough to realize that after a talk with you I know more about important matters than if I just tried to figure it out by myself."
- "What do you think of the idea of seeing if we can come to a conclusion that would allow us to each gain something, rather than argue it out and gain nothing?"

These manners of expression convenience a loosening effect whereby each mate is more likely to be inclined to lighten up long enough to find some truth to the other's position. Don't cut off your nose to spite your face. Instead, cut out the ego food that feeds the insistence of being right all the time. Admitting that you are sometimes off target in your opinions and decisions will help keep your bead on the target of maintaining and sustaining your love life. Exchange false pride for love and feast upon rather than insist upon this more harmonious manner of relating within your love relationship.

Note. From *Head Over Heart in Love: 25 Guides to Rational Passion* by Bill Borcherdt. Copyright © 1996, Professional Resource Exchange, Inc., P.O. Box 15560, Sarasota, FL 34277-1560.

Playing God and
Fighting Like the Devil:
When Love Falters

Practically all love relationship problems are a reflection of emotional problems and usually include the following scenes:

Scene 1 - Partner #1 displeases partner #2.

Scene 2 - Partner #2 takes a bad situation and makes it worse by foolishly angering himself about the original frustration.

Scene 3 - In a monkey-see, monkey-do fashion, partner #1 equally as foolishly disturbs herself about partner #2's anger toward her.

Scene 4 - The act is completed with an amplifying, multiplying effect. The original upset is mass-produced with both actors trying to make each other over - playing God and fighting like the devil at the same time. They then blame and damn each other for their upset, rather than taking responsibility for tripping their own emotional trigger. Finally, resentfulness and vindictiveness are allowed to linger. Hardly a sequence within which love can bloom!

Perhaps a bit of bending without breaking while accepting that the hardest thing to give in a relationship is to "give in" would do better. Simply stated, making a go of a love relationship boils down to overreacting to one another less and accommodating each other more - in that order. Rational emotive behavior therapy teaches to first upset yourself less about what you don't like in your love relationship *before* tackling the behavioral changes that will result in it running on all eight cylinders (or more accurately put, on *more* cylinders; any interaction between humans is far less than perfect). In efficiently building a case for tolerance, changes in the relationship system can more effectively and clearheadedly take place.

In truth, the seeds of love's failures are often planted at the time a love bond is established. Most participants in love's enterprises take a commercialized view of the matter and fall in love for the wrong reasons. Like the foolish person who built his house on the sand, love endeavors get off on the following wrong feet:

1. *As a childish excuse to demand reciprocation.* Love's attachments make the world go around; it's the demand for return attachments that causes dizziness (e.g., "I'll love you, I'll give you the best days of my life, I'll slobber all over you with the understanding that you slobber back all over me, and if you don't, I'll hate your guts until the day you die - and I hope it's soon"). This is true love at its frequently commercialized worst.
2. *To prove oneself.* Most people think they are a better person with love in their life. Consequently they go after the right thing (love) for the wrong reasons (ego, self-proving). The result is a lot of frantic efforts to control one another to establish alleged worth. Unfortunately, desperate people don't blend very well together.

Try to weave the following rational philosophies into your everyday thinking about your love life and see if you can live *not* happily ever after, but happier.

1. Honestly seek out your Godlike philosophies and dispute them. Ideas such as, "Thou shalt have no other val-

ues before mine," "My partner has my will - not free will," "My values are sacred and therefore my partner has no right to trespass on them," will have you fighting like the devil, discovering that when you win the battle you are likely to lose the war - and the love relationship.

2. Give your partner undamning acceptance. Condemn the sin if you wish, but don't condemn the sinner. The best way to influence people isn't to tell them how you think they should, must, or have to act, but to instead accept them the way they are.

3. Emphasize increasing your own low frustration tolerance. Use your love life to work on your own mental health. Heed Mohammed's words: "Tell me a mountain has moved and I'll believe, tell me a person has changed his character and I'll believe not." Whether we like it or not, most of the traits we don't like about our loved ones don't change very much. "My, how you have changed since I've changed" might be a more realistic view.

4. Don't make a point to look for the worm in the apple of your eye. Push yourself to focus on those features that you appreciate most in your loved one. Train yourself to warm the cockles of your heart in this way.

5. Drink to and not because of your loved one. Openly applaud to your partner and to others what you believe to be his or her strengths. Adopt the philosophy that you can attract more bees with honey than with vinegar.

6. Be more interested in understanding the other than getting the other to understand you. Avoid the attitude, "First I'll tell you my side of the story, then I'll tell you yours."

7. See yourself as an enjoying person in your own right. Don't depend on your love life to make you happy. Take on many nonloving interests. Don't put all your eggs in one love-life basket.

8. Be more interested in accommodating the relationship than in being right - lest it die with its rights on.

9. See that you don't "let" your partner do things. Due to free will, what your partner does is up to him or her.

Your choice is whether you are going to hassle your partner about what he or she decides.

10. See your contributions to the relationship as in your self-interest. The less you overreact to and the more you accommodate your partner the more fun you are likely to find your partner to be around.

11. Accept that falling in love is natural, but to maintain it is not naturally easy; that you fall in love but work your way into happiness.

Note. From *Head Over Heart in Love: 25 Guides to Rational Passion* by Bill Borcherdt. Copyright © 1996, Professional Resource Exchange, Inc., P.O. Box 15560, Sarasota, FL 34277-1560.

Love Versus Need:
Getting a Grip -
But Not Too Tight -
On Your Love Life

Narrow definitions of love abound, including:

- "If you love me, you are obligated to me."
- "If you love me, you won't say no."
- "If you love me, you will always agree with me."
- "If you love me, you will always understand me."
- "If you love me, you will never look at another man/woman."
- "If you love me, you will always put me first in everything."
- "If you love me, you will never criticize me."
- "If you love me, you will always encourage me."

This list could go further, but none would top the childish demand behind, "If you love me you will need me as I need you." Neediness isn't at the core of all of love's problems - just most. "Hang on for dear life and love, dear" may seem the solution to staying together, but instead introduces the problem. Humans are very quick to insist that if something is good, such as love, then they most certainly "need" it and "have to" have it. Reflected in our general cultural belief system, including in practically all theories of human behavior practiced by psychotherapists from the east to the west, is the claim that human beings have "needs" that unless met will cause dire emotional consequences. This tight-fitting way of thinking tightens rather than loosens up relationships, and as a result, participants lose out.

In a rational sense, love means getting close to somebody but then being able to let go when it is in one's best interest. Irrational "needs" mean not being able to get close to someone or getting close to someone but not being able to let go when the situation calls for it. By the looks of the world of love and the shape it's in, with so many people not being able to get close, or being able to get close but not let go, there is much room to question the conventional wisdom that says that all the world "needs" is love. Some of the negative emotional fall-out and practical complications that often result from a philosophy of neediness include:

1. *Gripping too hard leads to griping too much.* When you insist that another provide you what you allegedly need, much griping and complaining is likely to follow if such provisions are not granted (e.g., "Can't you see that my knuckles are white from clinging to what I need from you? By your not providing these necessities you're making me miserable, and I'm going to whine from now until the cows come home or until you deliver my necessities, whichever comes first").

2. *Drives your social group away.* Getting yourself hung up on your "needs" preoccupies you, you, you with a me, me, me mentality that will make you miserable to be around, miserable to be around, miserable to be around.

3. *Focuses on fusing with another rather than having fun with another.* Playfulness is lost when the goal becomes to join with the identity of another rather than establish your own.

4. *Distracts from giving love.* When the main concern is to get love the value of giving it is slighted. In that one of the best ways to get love is to give it in a nondesperate way, a valuable resource for opening up its doors is lost.

5. *Results in reaping what you sow.* Planting the seeds of limited, needful thinking harvests crops of restrictive, desperate living later on. Entering a relationship reeking with "neediness" and as a means of "meeting my needs" often results in leaving the relationship empty-handed and empty-headed.

6. *Subtracts from personality well-roundedness.* A very limited view of self and life results from the one-dimensional view of needing love, and nothing else will do. Other things that you could be doing to enjoy life are never tested due to your fanatical, all-love-or-nothing perspective.

7. *Puts pressure on all concerned.* Compulsively locking yourself into your love life, without consideration of other enjoying options puts a lot of responsibility on you to obtain what you have determined as necessary, and heavy expectations on your partner to provide for your demands.

8. *Especially burdens the stronger partner.* After all, if you are the strong one and the one person for me, the weak one, and if you forsake me, I am likely to conclude that you are responsible for doing me in by disappointing me. The burden of looking after someone who makes himself or herself near totally dependent upon another may prompt the stronger party to leave before being weakened as energy is sapped by the bottomless pit of the dependee.

9. *Prompts proving self rather than being self.* Declaring that you need love from someone will likely set plans in motion to prove yourself. This strategy will often backfire in that efforts to impress another distract from showing an active, sincere interest in them.

10. *Will cause you to be more interested in what others can do for you and in their understanding you, than in what they can do for themselves, in what you can do for them, and in your understanding them.* Due to its obnoxious qualities, self-centeredness is a trait that encourages others to center their thinking away from you.

11. *Results in mutual resentment.* Being asked to sacrifice your general life's ambitions to devote yourself to your needy partner sparks long-range animosity. Not getting a return on your demands for undivided attention from your loved one leads to resentment as well.

12. *Encourages the commercialization of a natural state.* Humans are raised in a social group and therefore naturally bond with one another. The minute the drama button is pushed by creating a seeming "need" for attachment, a soap opera way of coping is set in gear. These disturbed methods are reinforced by the cultural prescription for handling such disappointing matters; that is, getting up on your soap box and declaring how, in light of your partner not supplying your demands for a return attachment, you intend to harm him/her, yourself, or both of you. Such irrational methods of self-management are portrayed in movies, on television, and in other media as the automatic response to "need" deficiencies. This dramatic style may sell more tickets at the movies, but it doesn't remedy a disappointment being turned into disaster and emotional disorder.

13. *Sets the stage for betrayal.* Attempts to forcefully pull your partner toward you ripens the possibility that such dominance will result in pushing him or her in the opposite direction - right into the arms of another.

14. *Prompts nauseatingly ingratiating and smothering conduct on your part.* Bending over backwards to please by seeing how many times and with how much excess gratitude you can pacify your mate is a cover-up for (a) fear of not being able to find the right ridge on your mate's feet and lick it enough times to neutralize the power you believe he or she has over you, and (b) frantic efforts to treat the other so excessively accommodatingly that he or she couldn't possibly find any reason for leaving such a patronizing person as you.

15. *Helps establish avoidance if not exclusion patterns of relating.* Hovering over someone is akin to suffocating them. Needy-acting people burn out the bond they so exceed-

ingly wish to establish; due to their obnoxious, clinging antics, they find themselves alone much of the time.

16. *Creates jealousy and possessiveness.* Fear of losing one's lifeline prompts controlling efforts that often result in losing control of your love life. Childish insistences that your partner structure your time by ongoing hand-holding will likely lead to losing a grip on what you value.

17. *Restricts options.* Painting yourself into a corner by relying solely on your loved one for desirable provisions leaves you with only one choice in a world that requires more than one choice to survive and thrive.

18. *Causes stewing and brooding, not doing.* Needfulness creates worry about losing your defined emotional lifeline. Worrisome activity in the form of sitting on your behind while making yourself a prisoner of your own obsessive mind is likely to follow.

19. *Sometimes provides a quick fix without being fixed.* Feeling better and getting better are two different things. Neediness and fearfulness can be temporarily perfumed by your partner complying with your needful demands. Such quick accommodation feels good, but you will get worse in that your emotional dependency is reinforced by your partner's provisions. Sucking from a pacifier is comforting in the short run but does not breed emotional self-reliance in the long run.

20. *Neediness is never-ending.* Needy-acting people are bottomless pits. No matter how much you temporarily satisfy their cravings for love, they are never satiated. Enough is never enough; in fact, too much is not enough.

21. *Can trigger verbal and emotional abuse.* When people are afraid, they tend to fight or flee. Attacking the person who, by your distorted, dependent way of thinking is destroying you by refusing to provide for your sacred "needs" is an all-too-common method of intimidation designed to force them to do so.

22. *Prompts fear.* Needy-acting people are fearful people. They are afraid about the possibility of you sweeping the rug out from under them, leaving them without emo-

tional supplies. The problem here is that one of the surest ways to fail is to make yourself afraid of the possibility of failing.

23. *Often leads to self- or other blame.* Putting yourself down for being an emotional cripple or blaming another for your dependency handicap are common methods of coping with emotional unsureness.

24. *Can cultivate self-pity.* "Poor me that you, as the supplier of my deserved needs, is ceasing to provide them" - this is the sometimes battle cry of the emotionally wounded dependent one.

25. *Mixes the issue of sharing your life with and sacrificing your life for another.* Being concerned about sharing your life with someone you love is different from consuming yourself about the other not being ready, willing, or able to sacrifice his or her life for you.

26. *Feeds upon a master-slave mind-set.* Efforts to mastermind for control make you the believed master of someone else who by your self-absorbed view has got nothing else better to do than to wait on you hand and foot so as to insure your nonstop comfort.

27. *Is a forerunner of hurt and hypersensitivity.* Putting all your eggs in one basket is risky in that it makes another's decision to attach or not attach to you an all-important, all-consuming matter.

28. *Results in poor performances in other areas of life.* Concentration and zest for other areas of life are lost due to preoccupation with your troublesome love life.

29. *Stems from and reinforces emotionally disturbed philosophies of:*

   - *Desperation.* Because desperate people don't blend well together, relationships are often lost before they get out of the starting gate.
   - *Necessitizing.* When what is established as nice is defined as necessary, the frantic tail begins to wag the dog.

- *Nonnegotiability.* When negotiable wants are blown up into nonnegotiable needs, possibilities for bargaining for more-well-thought-out solutions are lost.
- *Exaggeration.* Awfulizing about molehills will soon turn them into mountains too steep to climb for the purpose of salvaging your love life.
- *Compellingness.* Love based on compulsion - that is, "I have to have - you have to provide" - will wear thin hopes for other than a strained and strife-filled relationship.
- *Demandingness.* All or nothing, only this way or only that way, my way as the only way puts unrealistic demands on your partner and on your relationship with him or her. As a result, you tighten yourself up rather than lighten yourself up.

30. *Takes away your potential of putting your best foot forward.* Emotional dependency will paint you into the opposite picture that you want to become. Needful-acting people act unstable. They fall all over themselves, leaving others unimpressed. As a result of their declared need for love, they appear as lovable as a wet mop. They defeat the purpose of what it is they are trying too hard to accomplish.

Trying too hard to hang on for dear life, dear often is the deathbed of love. Too strongly tightening your grip on your love life reflects personal weakness and insecurity, whereas loosening the same grip reveals emotional strength and self-confidence. Getting closer in your love life often means coming to terms with the value of loosening your grip on it. Develop a philosophy of "If I want you to keep loving me and if I want to keep loving you, best we see that we don't need each other." Such a lighter grip may well lead to less griping, which in turn frees you up to promote more loving.

Note. From *Head Over Heart in Love: 25 Guides to Rational Passion* by Bill Borcherdt. Copyright © 1996, Professional Resource Exchange, Inc., P.O. Box 15560, Sarasota, FL 34277-1560.

Fight With Me
Or You Don't Love Me:
Refusing the
Misery-Likes-Company Invite

Humans sometimes find comfort in others' discomfort, especially if they contribute to the other's misery bank. There are several reasons for this:

1. By contrasting another's unhappiness with your own, one can gleefully conclude to not having it so bad after all. In this sense, the comparative analysis becomes a comforting coping mechanism.
2. A smug, peculiar sense of satisfaction can be experienced when observing another's misery that one provided the stimulus for.
3. "Sharing the wealth" of misery with someone seems to dilute its impact on the sender.
4. A sense of power and control is gained from promoting your undesirable state of mind while successfully prompting your partner to take on a likewise unhappy emotional state.
5. Ego replenishment. If I see myself as a "bad person" for having a "bad," unhappy state of mind, I can at least conclude that I am not as bad as you, or at least you are equally as bad as me for taking on similar emotional rough going.

Application of this misery-likes-company philosophy also has significant drawbacks, especially when used in the context of a love relationship. Examples are:

1. The more the unmerrier. With one person in a duo being unhappy, the relationship is far less likely to be overrun with disenchantment. Simple mathematical calculations will tell you that two is worse than one when it comes to not being able to put to rest feelings of distress.
2. Resentfulness springs up when partner number one realizes that he or she has allowed himself or herself to be had by partner number two's encouragement to sign his or her name on the dotted line of misery.
3. Few appreciate being "hustled" by another's scheme to contribute to a poisoning of their mental health. A loss of respect for the sender of such a low blow often follows such a manipulative plot.
4. Contributes to a monkey-see, monkey-do relationship pattern. The idea, "Okay, if you're going to purposefully annoy me just because you feel especially annoyable, then I will do the same with you when the misery-likes-company shoe is on the other foot," is a view that is commonly installed in future interactions.

Feelings of betrayal are often made to follow when the misery invitation is turned down. It is as if the unhappy partner is implying, "If you really loved me, you would join me in my misery." Such immature suggestions are best countered with, "If you really loved me you would be happy for me that I'm not as unhappy as you." Mature love consists of wishing your partner well, and being happy for him or her - even when you're not happy yourself.

The following are common methods used when misery wants company. Thoughts that will counter these sleek maneuvers will follow. Alert yourself to the following strategies often employed as attempted and tempting misery-induction devices:

1. *Reworking sore spots.* Personal sensitivities picked at can open up old, unhappy wounds - if you let them.
2. *Raking your past mistakes over the coals.* Aggressively reminding you of any or all errors in judgment is an attempt to get under your emotional skin.
3. *Sly comments about others' negative comments.* Your partner unfairly mentioning that he or she overheard someone else criticize you is a tricky means of inviting you to go for the gossipy bait. People who tell such tales out of school are usually trying to provide themself with consolation for their own boredom and despair.
4. *Nitpicking.* Trivial complaints about your manner are a tip-off for larger dissatisfactions in the other's own flaws.
5. *Finger pointing.* Your partner's harshly blaming you for his or her own problems and disturbances represents a lack of responsibility for self and an attempt to pass the buck of emotional disturbance.
6. *Attacking disagreements.* Angering oneself about ever-present individual differences of opinion reflects a cover-up for personal insecurity and a fearful state of mind triggered by emotional dependency. Fear and insecurity are disguised by such hostile attacks.
7. *Self-pity demonstrations.* Sulking when not getting one's own way can be an attempted effort to prompt you to frustratingly attempt the impossible task of saving your partner from himself or herself.
8. *Attempted guilt induction.* See that by directly implying that love and obligation go hand in glove, your mate is trying to pass the baton of upset to you; that is, you "should" fill his or her request and if you were really in love, you would.

Use the following rational self-statements to prevent yourself from (a) embittering yourself about your partner's attempts to use your emotional well-being to cushion flaws in him or her and (b) going for the unhappiness transfer strategy itself:

- "Better that I not foolishly get myself upset about my partner's attempts to pique my interest in being unhappy."
- "How unfortunate that my loved one wishes me to be as upset as he is; for both our good let me see how I can prevent that from happening."
- "Offer compassion not company."
- "Don't go for the bait."
- "Do both of us a favor by backing off rather than blowing up."
- "Don't trip your own trigger just because it has been requested that you do so."
- "Love and obligation are not one and the same."
- "Because my loved ones would like the honor of my presence at their misery doesn't mean I am required to accept the invitation."
- "Perhaps the most loving thing that I can do for my loved ones is to not take them as seriously as they are taking themselves."
- "Duplicating their overreaction will only take a bad situation and make it worse."

Lead yourself not into the temptation of the misery-likes-company trap. Instead deliver yourself from evil by replacing "fight with me if you love me" with "I won't fight with you because I do love you." Passing on the invitation to share in misery invites a more loving manner of companionship with your loved one.

Note. From *Head Over Heart in Love: 25 Guides to Rational Passion* by Bill Borcherdt. Copyright © 1996, Professional Resource Exchange, Inc., P.O. Box 15560, Sarasota, FL 34277-1560.

The Hard Side of
Love Makes It Easier

In life and love it is often not easy to take the easy way out. Little is gained in the long run without first accepting pain in the short run. While setting boundaries in and regulating love relationships are often difficult to do today, they frequently prevent tomorrow's misunderstandings and disputes. Narrow definitions of love and caring block a long-range view of what makes relationships tick. The idea that if you love someone you are to always take the line of least resistance in pleasing them fails to establish important conditions in a love relationship. Thinking that if you love someone you won't say "no" to their requests, that you are to put the other first and yourself a distant - or at most a close - second practically all the time, that you are to endlessly encourage the other's development at the expense of your own, or that it's important that you upset yourself about your loved one's problems and disturbances leaves no rules to violate. This is a violation of the future of the relationship in that it reflects a relationship that is unable to stand the test of controversy - and likely unable to stand the test of time.

Burying your head in the sand with an "anything goes" philosophy leaves the relationship without a foundation of values from which to build. Standing up for yourself by unangrily letting your partner know that you stand for something will increase the chances your love life won't fall because it has nothing to structure itself with. Drawing a line in the sand while standing up and being counted by defining those conditions under which you are willing to stay together and those under which you would rather switch than fight gives you more bargaining power and your relationship more hope. Giving your partner a blank check may provide the short-range comforts of conflict avoidance but result in relationship bankruptcy in the long run.

Lacking concern about pleasing or displeasing one's partner leaves the relationship without a sense of anticipation and participation as take-for-grantedness and complacency are allowed to set in. By not establishing leverage you put yourself in a weaker bargaining position. If you repeatedly give your mate his or her own way, motivation to contribute is lost. After all, if one can have one's cake and eat it too, while losing weight besides, what incentive is there to diet? When couples know what is expected of one another they are in a better position to make those accommodating provisions.

The following suggestions are designed to promote a finer appreciation for what those provisions are, leading to a more general appreciation of the relationship. When a twosome realizes that neither will be allowed to take advantage of the other, mutual respect is more easily established. When elbow grease is required to accommodate one and compromise with another, pride in the relationship is more likely to be established. Hard work today makes the job easier while breeding fuller appreciation tomorrow. Using the hard side of love to make it easier includes:

1. Don't take responsibility for the other's problems and upsets. Practice humility by accepting the human limits in transplanting an attitude into your partner's head or a feeling into his or her gut. There are things that you can't do for others - they can only do for themselves. To attempt such impossible missions will likely make love harder due to your not accepting the reality that when your partner is upsetting himself or herself there is often hardly anything that you can do about it.

2. Don't lift a finger when it would encourage another's do-nothingism. Avoid picking up after others as they will likely expect such favors indefinitely into the future. Someone once said, "Give a person a fish and he will eat for today, teach him how to fish and he will eat for a lifetime." Doing others' chores may help them to breathe easier today, but they will likely never develop the stamina to carry their own weight for a lifetime. Such an imbalance is a long-range breeding ground for dependency and mutual resentment.

3. Tell how you think and feel without telling the other off. Be firm and no-nonsense in your tone and message as to what you're willing and not willing to contribute to the relationship. However, leave anger out of your tactics of expression or you will discourage your mate from hearing your message behind the fire in your eyes.

4. Say no when it is in your best interest to do so. Don't accommodate to a fault. Refusing another's request at the appropriate time not only protects you from unwanted intrusion of your time but it also communicates to the requester a vote of confidence; that he or she is not an emotional cripple and therefore is capable of handling in an accepting way a thumbs-down on his or her request.

5. Don't take others as serious as they are taking themselves. Pitying others puts them in a one-down position. Caringness need not be defined by how much emotional drama you throw on your loved ones' concerns. Taking others less seriously than they are taking themselves is an act of love and kindness in that it encourages others to give themselves the same type of emotional slack about their problems that you are giving to them.

6. Take on nonloving interests. Building in time for yourself and insisting that it remain even when your partner may not totally approve prevents you from putting all your loving eggs in one basket. The less dependent you make yourself on your love life the more love and out-

side activity you will be able to bring into that relationship to spice it up.

7. Behavioral trade-offs, not blank checks. "I'll scratch your
    back if you scratch mine" means just that. "I'll do favors
    for you but only if you do some for me" lessens
    one-sidedness and its eventual animosity pitfalls.

8. Consistent leveling. Not beating around the bush by di-
    rectly posing and positioning your preferences, desires,
    and intentions provides opportunity for more clear-cut,
    well-thought-out decisions by your mate.

9. Avoid caregiving to a fault by caring less without be-
    coming uncaring. Don't give it the limp hand by looking
    the other way about your partner's distress. Don't go to
    the opposite extreme of trying to do your partner's work
    for him or her. Rather, appreciate that emotional involve-
    ment without entanglement is the key distinction between
    a good doer and a do-gooder.

10. Withhold love and affection when treated harshly. Show
    your loved one that there is no free lunch and that there
    is an entry fee for viewing and experiencing your warmth
    and kindness. Show that your love is to be earned, thus
    encouraging mutual respect, an important ingredient in
    determining whether love lasts.

11. Use selective inattention. Firmly refuse to respond to
    third-degree questions as well as those topics that con-
    sistently lead to locking horns in disagreement. Directly
    explain to your partner that you're willing to talk about
    less-blaming and less-controversial topics but not thorn-
    in-the-side matters.

12. Clearly share; decidedly don't sacrifice. Make it as plain
    as the nose on your mate's face that you are eagerly and
    enthusiastically ready, willing, and able to share in the
    good that your relationship has to offer. Make it equally
    as clear that you are not willing to sacrifice or compro-
    mise your values for the other, lest in the long run you
    make yourself so resentful that you might punch that
    same nose on his or her face!

13. Explain how nice it is to give *and* receive. Document that you aren't in this relationship for nothing. Rather, that you want provisions from it; that you are willing to provide your partner with a profit, but that you too expect certain gains and advantages.

14. Set staunch conditions regarding vital aspects of the relationship as you see them. Some examples of possible nonallowed factors in the relationship would be, no physical or verbal abuse, no bankruptcy spending, no employment shiftlessness, and no infidelity.

15. Tell your loved ones that you are more interested in being understood than in them proving themselves right - and that you too will shoot for this target of wanting to be understood rather than disproving another.

16. State your distaste for unsolicited advice and that you also will do more asking than telling in matters of opinion; for instance, "What do you think?" versus "Don't you think?" or "Why don't you. . . ?"

17. Don't compromise to a fault. Be willing to bend on your points of view so long as you don't stretch your tolerance level beyond what you're willing to contend with over time.

18. Encourage your partner's interests by persuading him or her that his or her individual pleasuring interests are good for the both of you. If your partner is happier, this contributes to your own happiness, in that it's more enjoying to be around a happy camper.

19. Accept no false promises. If the goods can be delivered, fine. If not, best this be reckoned with sooner rather than later. That way false hopes that are dashed will not be allowed to stand in the way of the relationship.

20. Don't look the other way regarding inevitable personality and value distinctions. Agreeing to disagree is a more helpful method of coping with differences than sweeping them under a rug. Remind yourself that love and agreement need not be one and the same.

21. When necessary, remind your mate that love and obligation do not go hand in glove. Because you love your

partner does not mean you are required to honor his or her every request.

22. Explain to your loved one that your decisions to accommodate or to not accommodate reflect you being for your values and not you being against him or her.

23. Decisively take a time-out or enormously detach to avoid heated arguments. Literally take a step or more back and when necessary leave the fighting arena in order to avoid heavy-duty, relationship-defeating friction.

24. Review the grim reality that because you love someone you will always understand the one you love. Forthrightly yet patiently explain to your mate the limits of your understanding and that such deficiency on your part does not reflect your lack of love for him or her.

25. Strongly suggest that you and your partner use the ABC's of Rational Emotive Behavior Therapy's emotional reeducation to interrupt your emotional upsets. Thus, when you sense that the two of you are starting to raise your emotional temperatures with one another take the lead in outlining how your overreactions at "C" (emotional consequences) do not result from "A" (adversity or activating event) but rather directly from your "Bs" (belief systems). Encourage more responsibility for each of your emotions by tracking down those specific irrational beliefs/strongly stated self-sentences (e.g., "You're making me angry," "You have no right to address me in this negative manner - how awful that you are," and "How bad you are for acting so badly"). Then, refinish your irrational belief structure with different, more tolerant, accepting ideas at "D" (different way of thinking, debate, dispute; e.g., "I'm upsetting myself - now how can I think in a way so as to upset myself less?," "You have free will, not my will," and "Your acts may be bad, but you're not bad"), so that at "E" you can produce more favorable feelings or emotional effects. By using the ABC's of emotional understanding and change structure you can use your differences to work yourself into improved mental health. By vigorously challenging yourselves to give each

other "undamning acceptance," what appears to be a liability can be made into an asset.

Setting the record straight today, doing it right now in spite of whatever difficulty it takes to do so will likely make life and loving easier tomorrow in that errors due to neglect won't be required to be undone. Being hard without being harsh, and by showing displeasure when expectations are violated will encourage you and yours to feast upon the reality that not only may you easily fall in love, but with much hard work you stand an easier chance of working yourself into happiness.

Note. From *Head Over Heart in Love: 25 Guides to Rational Passion* by **Bill Borcherdt**. Copyright © 1996, Professional Resource Exchange, Inc., P.O. Box 15560, Sarasota, FL 34277-1560.

Hitting Below the Belt:
Where and Why It Really Hurts
Love's Intentions

Low blows are a form of foul play that blocks playing for keeps in intimate relationships otherwise worth keeping. Harshly laced comments are about as quick a way to guarantee relationship failure as one could find. Yet, using another's sore spots or "Achilles' heel" as ammunition to accompany your argument is a frequent means of trying to do your mate in. The problem is that with such dirty-pool tactics you lose when you win. After associating with someone for a period of time you will likely notice which references to them lead to their raising the hair on their head en route to raising the roof! Humans often make themselves emotionally allergic to pet negative comments directed toward them. The trick is to avoid such critical references in the service of salvaging and sustaining the relationship. If the other would be allergic to strawberries you likely would not feed them strawberries. Avoiding mean comments like the plague contributes to not plaguing your future in the relationship. Examples of such prickly comments are:

- "That new outfit looks nice on you - especially since you're 30 pounds heavier than the day we got married."
- "Which member of your family do you think you got your big nose from?"
- "You have always had difficulty with math, haven't you."

- "You're just like your mother/father."
- "You always act childishly when you don't get your own way."
- "You've been divorced twice now, right?"
- "Temper, temper."
- "You've missed out on that promotion three times now, haven't you."
- "What's it like to be balding/graying?"

Following are some possible motivations for such calculated comments, along with the irrational ideas (IIs) that propel them and the countering beliefs (CBs) that will prevent their destructive use.

1. *A mechanism of filling a dire need to control and dominate.*

    II: "I have to control my relationships with significant others, and one of the quickest ways to access such dominance is to wave a red flag in front of them."
    CB: "When I attack to gain control I lose relationships."

2. *As expressions of spite, revenge, and vindictiveness.*

    II: "I'll throw mud in their eye; that way I'll teach them a lesson they won't soon forget. Then they will be sure to never cross me again."
    CB: "Bittersweet revenge - who needs it? Best I get wise, not get even, lest I make myself an open target for a return of their mudslinging."

3. *For the purpose of self-proving.*

    II: "I have to prove my absolute superiority over others, and one manner of accomplishing this psychological one-up-personship is to get under their skin."
    CB: "By trying to put myself one-up I am merely contributing to the relationship going down the tubes."

4. *As an effort to mask feelings of insecurity and inferiority.*

II: "I secretly believe myself to be a second-class citizen, so to shake these insecurities I'll maliciously tie into others' shortcomings. Such reminders to them help me to forget my own inadequacies and deficiencies."

CB: "The best way to overcome rather than be overrun by discontents about myself is to accept myself in spite of them - not to condemn others for their disappointments of self."

5. *To give vent to demands for social acclaim and approval.*

II: "I have to present myself in a way that will impress my social group. A sure way to do that is to bring to their attention those traits that I am totally unimpressed with in others."

CB: "I don't have to make myself into such a screwball with such an emotional bottomless pit that I can't help myself in desperately trying to gain others' favorable impressions."

6. *As an antiboring activity.*

II: "Life is so drab. The only way I can think of to spice it up is to try to get an emotional rise out of others by not so discreetly reminding them of what they are self-conscious about."

CB: "There are better ways to get a rise out of life than at the expense of others. Such malicious sarcasm will only cause my love life to falter if not fail."

7. *As an expression of low frustration tolerance (LFT).*

II: "I can't stand so many things about my mate and I just have to point out his flaws or I'll just emotionally burst at the seams."

CB: "Better that I use my disfavors about others to work on my mental health by building a case for tolerance and acceptance of them."

8. *As a means of camouflaging feelings of hurt.*

II: "She hurt me by some of her past negative criticisms and behaviors, so I'll give her a dose of her own medicine by kicking into gear some anger I can directly throw at her."

CB: "Nobody can hurt me but me. I took my partner's past negative criticisms and behaviors too seriously and hurt myself by my personalizing and over-reactions to his antics. I need not get myself bogged down in such misinterpretations of my own feelings."

9. *As a manner of advancing smugness.*

II: "I feel pretty good about everything in my life and have every right to flaunt my coziness by reintroducing to others their believed problems and limitations."

CB: "Best I build myself a life based on continuing anticipation and participation. By striving for other things in my life I'll be too stimulated and active to give others a hassle about their felt peculiarities."

10. *As an attempt to use good teasing intentions not backed by the right methods.*

II: "If I hassle and tease him enough about what he embarrasses himself easily about, perhaps he will feel shamed enough to change."

CB: "Better that I support my partner's strengths than try to teasingly exploit her weaknesses. That way I may be able to leave a more affirmative mark on her views."

Hitting below the belt, picking at another's sore spots, antagonizes and hurts long-range goals of increased love and compatibility. Its opposite, a decent respect for and acceptance of human limitations, can go a long way in establishing love connections. Mustering up the restraint to not pick at another's self-conscious views links up emotionally nourishing good intentions with the right, supportive methods. In this way love's intentions will purposefully and intentionally be made to better strive and thrive.

Note. From *Head Over Heart in Love: 25 Guides to Rational Passion* by Bill Borcherdt. Copyright © 1996, Professional Resource Exchange, Inc., P.O. Box 15560, Sarasota, FL 34277-1560.

Mind Reading: Hazards of Thinking You Know More About Others Than They Know About Themselves

In the midst of a marital counseling session, the female partner abruptly blurted, "I can tell he is angry right now." Since her partner seemed at ease with the contents of the session, I inquired in a perplexed tone, "How can you tell?" She quickly replied, "I can tell by the wrinkle on his brow." To her surprise, when I asked her mate if he was in fact feeling angry, he stated that although he often wrinkled his brow in the midst of concentrated thinking, he was not feeling angry. This case of mistaken feeling identity points to a common flaw in love relationships, in which one partner assumes to know more about the partner's thinking and feeling than the partner does. This love relationship wave length often leads to practical problems of:

1. Setting in motion a chain of misunderstandings. When original blindfolded assumptions are in error, additional calculations by either party will be off base too. Another will likely respond to you in the way you say you view them, and if your original hunch is wrong, the response is likely to be equally as half-baked.
2. People often resent being told what they are thinking, feeling, or doing. Mind reading implies that you have

more awareness of others than they have of themselves. They will often view your guesswork as an intrusion, and as with any intruder, they are likely to not take kindly to you. Consequently, not only are misunderstandings set in motion, but so are animosities created.

3. Encourages and reinforces the magical thinking that then furthers the mind-reading myth. Anyone who could read minds could get rich in the stock market. By trying to play God in seeing through another's thoughts and intentions, then convincing yourself that you really do have such mystical powers, you influence yourself to exercise future claims to this mystical ability.

4. Problem solving about actual problems gets lost in the shuffle. By quibbling about nonexistent accusations, valid real-life concerns do not get attended to. As a result, reality problems combine with the arguments about alleged matters to produce a sizable amount of relationship strife.

Avoiding the negative fall-out from hopeless attempts at gazing into another's thoughts while interpreting them for him or her can be done by applying the following suggestions:

1. Ask, don't tell. Most people prefer to be asked their opinion, not told it. "What do you think?" rather than "I know what you think" will go further in winning people and influencing friends than putting your words in someone else's mouth.

2. Check out your hunches *before* leading with them. Rather than cramming your noble notions down another's throat, first inquire as to their accuracy. "I have a suspicion," "I'm wondering if," or "I've got this hunch," with all three followed by, "and I'd like to check my notion out with you" will be more likely to prevent ill feelings than a more forceful explanation.

3. Get a larger database. Extend the conversation or activity further in an effort to gain additional information from which you can more accurately base your conclusions. A limited data sampling such as "the wrinkle on his

brow" mentioned earlier will likely not be as accurate as more extended observations of and happenings in the discussion.

4. Admit to the grandiosity behind your quick conclusions. Owning up to your high-and-mighty assumptions that you can tell something exists without any evidence to support its existence, except in your all-knowing head, is a prerequisite to your changing your superior stance.

5. Advance humility. Develop a decent respect for what you can and can't tell about another person. With a more down-to-earth perspective comes a more limited, though realistic, understanding of another.

6. Use qualifying words to yourself. "I think," "I guess," "My hunch is," and "I'm not sure, but" leaves a doubt on which to hang future information to the contrary. Otherwise, you will lock yourself into finalistic thinking that could prove fatal for the relationship.

7. Determine to not let your initial impressions be your guiding light. Draw more enlightened conclusions by making yourself open-minded enough to consider additional impressions beyond your first blush.

8. When in doubt - advance straightforwardness. Consider openly stating to your partner, "Rather than try to read your mind and draw premature or false conclusions, I'd like to be direct in checking something out with you." Honesty may not always be the best policy, but it often beats the heck out of beating around the bush.

9. Treat others the way you *and* they would like to be treated. Most people prefer that their mind not be inspected by another while being told what they are thinking. Fully appreciating how refreshing it is for you when others, instead of darting in and defining your thoughts for you, stay out of your way of thinking, will encourage you to provide others with the same latitude. Not meddling with others' mind's eyes is both a vote of confidence in others' ability to think for themselves and a show of respect for individual differences of opinion.

10. Listing and studying daily the advantages of resisting trying to do someone else's thinking for them, and the disadvantages such short-circuiting wave-length efforts have for your love life, can serve as a reminder to stop and think before you try to do someone else's thinking for them.

"If you want to know your opinion, I'll give it to you"; "First I'll tell you my side of the story, then I'll tell you yours," are statements that illustrate how forcing your thinking on others or proclaiming more knowledge of their thinking than they themselves have can be hazardous to your love life. Making yourself mindful of the value of avoiding such an imposing strategy will likely result in a more favorable reading of your relationship. Asking what others think rather than telling them what is on their mind allows you to concentrate more on understanding them through their eyes and not your hunches.

Note. From *Head Over Heart in Love: 25 Guides to Rational Passion* by Bill Borcherdt. Copyright © 1996, Professional Resource Exchange, Inc., P.O. Box 15560, Sarasota, FL 34277-1560.

Finger Pointing:
Why Alibis Don't Get the
Loving Job and Joy Done

To ask most humans to admit wrongdoing is like asking for the moon. To ask and get them to tell you where you went wrong is a piece of cake. Nowhere is this human tendency to believe the worst in everyone except oneself (in which case one is filled with excuses and alibis) more obvious than in the work and play of love relationships. It is almost as if the more two people get to know each other the more difficult it is for them to face up to one another the facts of their errors and blunders. Perhaps this is because the more bonded humans become, the more dependent they tend to make themselves on being right in their loved one's eyes. As a consequence of their fear of appearing wrong, if not weak, they anger themself when confronted the least little bit with the extremely remote possibility that they have a flaw or two! What is made to follow is argument and mutual blame that blocks the work and play that go into making a go of love.

Finger pointing occurs when two people debate the merits of their differing individual positions on a topic with their goal being not to solve the problem, but to prove they're right and their partner wrong in their views of the problem. This "I'm the good guy and you're the bad guy" position is defensive and self-serving, and poorly serves the problem-solving efforts of a relationship. Areas in which finger pointing fails to promote desirable features in a love relationship include:

1. *Forsakes responsibility for self, without which very little can be changed.* Until one's part in the problematic plot is admitted, both feet are outside of the door, rather than the one foot being in the door of personal change that comes from owning rather than disclaiming fault.

2. *Encourages your loved one's denial and defensiveness.* The more you dig in your heels in proclaiming your absolute innocence in practically all matters, the more your partner will be encouraged to fight denial with more denial. Two little angels with no admitted fault will not result in corrective action; as a result problems linger and fester.

3. *Discourages experimentation.* As long as being wrong is viewed as being a crime, efforts to do different things and to do things differently will be discouraged. When people try something for the first time they are likely to falter simply from lack of experience in the project. People are less likely to risk if they see themselves at risk, either through their own or through their mate's eyes.

4. *Conveniences resentment.* Bitterness is often made to set in by overreacting to and personalizing one's partner's continual stubborn refusal to own up to what is at times an obvious error in judgment.

5. *Doesn't distinguish between fault and blame.* When finger pointing, wrongdoers are denying fault for fear that if they admit their mistakes they would have to blame themselves for making them.

6. *Limits the scope of the relationship.* Relationship well-roundedness is lost in the muck of finger-pointing dominance in that guardedness and defensiveness often spread like wildfire; consequently couples find themselves overfocused on putting out accusatory fires to the neglect of more constructively heating up their relationship.

7. *Promotes a philosophy of problem-solving avoidance.* The more one avoids admitting being wrong out of fear of being wrong, the more that fear is strengthened. Problems swept under the rug or delegated to other blame will not go away by themselves.

8. *Reinforces emotional dependency.* The more you blame because of dependency on another to provide you with undying understanding and acceptance that you are totally right and he or she is totally wrong, the more you make yourself into an emotional cripple who has difficulty living with himself or herself unless your rightness and righteousness can be proven.

9. *Much truth goes undiscovered and unsaid.* Monopolizing discussions about differing opinions with self-proving rather than self- and solution-revealing ideas leaves usable, helpful ideas unrevealed.

10. *Practices bigotry and totalitarianism.* All-or-nothing thinking, the kind that reeks of "I'm 100% right and you're 100% wrong," dominates finger-pointing, self-proving arguments. Such a black-or-white method of thought can do little but divide up a relationship.

Below are concrete suggestions for avoiding such defensive, other-blame trappings with their conflict-resolution avoidances and responsibility for self-failings:

1. *Experiment with halting excuse making.* For 1 day, come to terms with your errors by not passing the buck of your responsibility for making them. It may feel comforting to blame others or circumstances for what was made to go wrong, but such denials won't lead to future successes.

2. *Identify common personal faults and give them special corrective attention.* List 5 to 10 frequent errors that reflect some of your personality flaws. Make it a point to lessen some of them. By doing so you will retrain yourself away from holding others accountable for your problems and upsets.

3. *Use transparency and openness procedures to develop an immunity to personalizing and disguising your mistakes.* By making it a point to publicly admit to your blunders, there will be less of a tendency to deny their existence. Repeated exposure of your shortcomings to your social

group will likely result in increased motivation to correct them.

4. *Take on a philosophy of fault finding within self, but nonblaming of self.* To err is human, to blame is, unfortunately, even more human. Interrupt the cycle of blame by focusing more on the correction of your problem without condemning yourself for having it.

5. *Give yourself the same compassionate advice you would likely give a friend who had made the same error.* By being compassionate with yourself for making a mistake, you will be less inclined to point the blaming finger at others. Self-acceptance in spite of your errors opens up the gates of accountability for and correction of them.

6. *Organize an exchange system.* Reward yourself for each incident of open acknowledgement and accountability and penalize yourself for each instance of finger pointing. Each time you openly express, "I was in error" or "I'm upsetting myself" provide yourself with something positive (e.g., one dollar toward purchasing something you find desirable or toward a favorite pleasure such as a meal at your favorite restaurant, a movie, etc.). When you come forth with a blaming position (e.g., "This is all your fault," "You're getting me upset"), your task will be to penalize yourself (e.g., subtract one dollar from your money allotted to your pleasures; get up an hour earlier the next day). Giving yourself something positive to work toward and something negative to avoid may prove to be just the tonic to help you to help yourself remain grounded in your responsibility for self.

7. *Keep an eye out for rational models.* Note others who do fairly well what you would like to master by way of personal accountability. Seek out how they view matters of errors of personal judgment and what sets them apart in matters of dealing with them in a responsible way.

8. *Firmly commit yourself to the emotionally liberating motto, "I'll change," not "I'll get you to admit that you have to change."* Putting yourself in the problem-solving driver's seat by doing what you can do to correct the matter, regardless

of whether others decide to identify their part in the plot, provides more hope and emotional leeway for the future.

9. *Weave into your everyday thinking philosophies of non-defensiveness, tolerance for, and acceptance of self and others in spite of wrongdoing, and forgiveness for either making a mistake or not being willing or able to admit it.* Clear-headedness is created from practicing such methods of rational thought, leading the way toward owning and correcting the problem.

10. *Debate against your defensive, other-blaming ideas.* Don't take the human tendency to blame sitting down. Stand up for your mental health by identifying some ideas that counter original intolerant, nonaccepting notions. Write out both sets of ideas, as illustrated below, reviewing them daily. Then, put them on tape and hear yourself go to bat for your self-responsibility. See if you can *forcefully* convince yourself of the rational content of the countering statements.

DEFENSIVE, FINGER-POINTING IDEAS	COUNTERING, RATIONAL PREMISES
• "What is she looking at me for? I didn't do anything wrong."	• "She looks like she thinks I may be in the wrong. Let me review my conduct and see if I am."
• "How can I wiggle my way out of this one?"	• "There's nothing to wiggle or squirm about, just because I was human enough to make a mistake."
• "If I admit I'm wrong, I'll be a weakling. How can I avoid becoming a bigger weakling than I already am?"	• "Admitting a blunder is a sign of strength, not weakness; personal security rather than insecurity."
• "My mate finding out that I made a mistake would be awful and dehumanizing."	• "What is so awful about my mate finding out that I was human enough to falter?"

DEFENSIVE, FINGER-POINTING IDEAS *(Cont'd)*	COUNTERING, RATIONAL PREMISES *(Cont'd)*
• "Disclosing wrongdoing puts me in a one-down position, which I absolutely couldn't stand."	• "Better that I avoid all appearances of psychological one-up- or one-down-personship if I wish to keep up with our relationship."
• "I must always appear to be strong, in charge, and right."	• "Trying to appear strong, in charge, and right all or any of the time is a burden I can easily do without."
• "Beat him to the punch before he beats me to it."	• "Beating my partner to the punch will only beat our relationship into the ground."
• "I have to defend myself, because if I don't no one else will."	• "Where is it written that I have to put myself on trial and be defended?"
• "Somebody has to be blamed - better her than me."	• "Is there a universal law that says I must continue the myth of essential blame?"
• "If I admit I was wrong, he will expect me to always do so in the future."	• "Why do I have to make myself afraid of what my mate might expect of me, either now or in the future?"

A wrongdoer is not just someone who has done something wrong, but also someone who has left something undone - such as admit to the wrongdoing. The double whammy - faltering, then failing to own up to being at fault - multiplies human error in that the original mistake is left unattended, causing a multiplying effect. Expand your horizons by pointing yourself away from alibis and excuses in an effort to put your finger on what you can do to promote the joys and to accomplish the jobs of love.

Note. From *Head Over Heart in Love: 25 Guides to Rational Passion* by Bill Borcherdt. Copyright © 1996, Professional Resource Exchange, Inc., P.O. Box 15560, Sarasota, FL 34277-1560.

Evening Up and Getting Even: Scorekeeping and Its Connection to Self-Pity

- "I started the conversation last time, this time it's your turn."
- "Who apologizes the most around here?"
- "Who in this household spends or contributes the most money?"
- "Who does the most work around here, anyway?"
- "Who remembers birthdays and anniversaries more?"
- "Who was the last one to shut the light off and whose turn is it now?"
- "Don't get mad, get even."

Tabulating answers to questions like the first five doesn't add up to a solid relationship built on pooling individual resources in the service of the long-range happiness and survival of the match. Rather, it reflects a petty mentality based on trying to prove who contributes more and is appreciated the least; in short, as an avenue to release feelings of self-pity. Eventually such "poor me" expressions are brought to the final statement above - getting even with someone you think has given you the short end of the stick.

What does it matter if one person in a love relationship attends more to certain domestic matters than the other? After all, didn't the two of you come together to pool your resources so that they add up to 100%? On some days the ratio of contributions may be 60/40 or 70/30. What does matter is that nitpicking about ever-present inequalities be put to rest. Otherwise, what is likely to be made to happen is petty bickering discouraging individual initiatives to contribute to matters of joint responsibility. The solution of achieving perfect balance in contributions to tasks and projects is made into additional problems due to the petty, demanding manner of approaching a united balance.

This is not to say that *consistent and dramatic* flaws in rotation and balance of who does what, and when, be overlooked. But it is suggested that in the majority of cases such tilted occurrences not be made into federal cases. If you have to scrutinize to identify such failings, it's probably not worth mentioning and certainly not worth carrying a grudge about.

Due to individual differences, one partner may be a more effective communicator and therefore more consistently take the lead in such endeavors; one mate might be a better money manager and therefore more frequently dominate such matters; one may more naturally recall upcoming special dates and events and take charge in those situations. Such leadership possibilities where one partner takes on the brunt of the effort required to tend to the matter are as many as there are dimensions to domestic living. In love relationships, two people unite to pool their resources in an effort to produce enough love and goodwill to make it worth each partner's while to carry on. This can better be accomplished when favorable contributions by each are allowed to be naturally interchangeable. Love is made to run smoother when a calculated and computerized accounting system is not allowed to interfere with the natural flow of the relationship; that is, when each does what comes more naturally to them in accomplishing upkeep of the relationship. These natural contributions are stalled by overemphasis on evening up, with the end result being angrily trying to get even. Scorekeeping has its roots in self-pity; the tip-off to such self-centered indulgence can be seen in the following choice-blocking ideas:

- "I always get the short end of the stick."
- "I apologized first last time, this time it's her turn."
- "I corrected the children yesterday, today he can."
- "Part of last month's check went toward some new clothes for her; this month I get to spend some money on myself."
- "Last holiday season we visited his parents, so this time around we have to visit mine."
- "She drove the new car last week, so this week it's my turn."
- "On our last vacation we did what he wanted, so this time I get my way."
- "I wrote everything down that she does around here, and everything that I do, and believe me I do more."
- "I shouldn't have to do any more than he does."
- "This relationship has to be evened up, and until it is I couldn't possibly be happy - in the meantime I won't get mad - just even."
- "I'll go on a sit-down strike just to show how mad I am that she is getting more out of this relationship than I am."
- "Woe is me, I contribute so much, and get less in return than my partner."

These self-statements are hung up on believed injustices; they had best be refinished with the following constructive ideas that can pave the way toward more acceptance of ever-present individual differences in relationship contributions:

- "Why is it so terrible if on certain days I contribute more than my fair share to keeping this relationship going?"
- "Stop thinking and acting like a 2-year-old just because you're not getting the long end of the stick!"
- "It's part of the human condition to be treated unfairly much of the time. Why do I have to be the one person who is immune from this reality?"
- "At times I may choose to tell my loved one my thoughts and feelings about what I am disappointed about, but that's a far cry from telling her off."
- "Give a little, take a little, gain a lot."

- "Better that I not exaggerate how bad I think I've got it or I'll whine my way right out of this relationship."
- "One of the hardest things about love is to give in. Yet, this might prove easier than being out of the relationship looking in, which may occur if I don't compromise."
- "Evening up puts me behind in my efforts to maintain my love life."
- "Poor me leads to a poor love life."

Scorekeeping can go on endlessly - if you let it. Adding up who does what, when, more often, and in a more extreme form and whose individual contributions are more noble than the other (e.g., "The fact that I do this is more worthy than any 10 things that you do") can border on the ridiculous. Better to avoid these numbers games of adding up the tab, because such definitions of unevenness will eventually connect with self-pity and resentment, putting a damper on if not disconnecting your love bond. Instead, sit down and agree that you each have worthwhile contributions to bring to the relationship and that you have strong intentions to carry forth with those provisions, but you are going to avoid nitpicking the quantity and quality of these resources in an effort to not only get even, but to get ahead in the game of love.

Note. From *Head Over Heart in Love: 25 Guides to Rational Passion* by Bill Borcherdt. Copyright © 1996, Professional Resource Exchange, Inc., P.O. Box 15560, Sarasota, FL 34277-1560.

Backhanded Compliments as Backdoor Aggression: Saying One Thing And Meaning Another

Keeping on the straight and narrow of what makes love tick requires steady, sincere effort. To keep what you have by way of love means staying between the lines of saying what you mean and meaning what you say in a complimentary way. Lax, sloppy thinking and the behavioral messages that follow reflect less caring and take-for-grantedness, and that will poison love possibilities. Anger and aggression come in various sizes and shapes. Whether expressed directly in the form of emotional or physical abuse or indirectly via some of the double messages illustrated below, goals of comfort and closeness are defeated. A unique example of this backhand method of expressing hostility would be the person who, after building a case for resentment, would express animosity by sloshing the mate's toothbrush around in the toilet!

Backhand compliments have a calculated hostile intent. Rather than use more civilized grievance procedures, the sender decides to opt for what usually turns out to be bittersweet revenge via sneaky, verbal underhandedness offerings such as:

- "You're a good parent - considering the family you came from."

- "You handled that situation gracefully - especially when you consider that you usually have two left feet."
- "The rest of you looks handsome - now if you could only do something about that nose."
- "I can see that you would rather be lucky than good."
- "You deserve first prize - in a poor person's beauty contest."
- "You look good - when I look the other way."
- "I appreciate it that you try so hard to be pleasantly kind to me - especially since you never succeed."
- "That was a great idea that you came up with - especially since it was the one that I came up with a long time ago."
- "You didn't have to help me out - but I appreciate the fact that you FINALLY did."
- "You sure came from a nice family - but did your parents ever have any children?"
- "You've got that natural look - too bad Mother Nature gave you such a raw deal."

All these backhanded comments say one thing but intend another. They often result in the receivers making themselves feel hurt, leading to their own brand of resentment. Compliments are underhandedly canceled out in favor of sly criticisms. Such behind-the-scenes words of bitterness establish an underlying critical structure for the relationship: one based on low-level, immature teasings. Under such an umbrella individuals often spend an abundance of time decoding messages or defensively trying to protect themself from their hostile content. They become a real burr in the saddle for those wishing for more pleasant contact.

To not get yourself caught up in these childish, eye-for-an-eye-and-tooth-for-a-tooth hostile teasings:

1. Honestly admit to their existence.
2. Just as honestly own up to the fact that you didn't simply come by them mysteriously, but that you created them.

3. Don't put yourself down for this flaw in your personality.
4. Take time to acknowledge and appreciate the negative effects such commentaries have on your love life.
5. Openly admit to your mate what you have been not so secretly doing while apologizing for your relationship-defeating misbehaviors.
6. Forthrightly voice your intention to do better in the future while actively soliciting your mate's assistance in giving you ongoing feedback about your efforts to change.
7. Use thought substitution as indicated below to assist you in keeping your commitment to do better.

THOUGHTS THAT CAUSE BACKDOOR AGGRESSION	THOUGHT SUBSTITUTES THAT WILL PREVENT BACKDOOR AGGRESSION
• "Just when he thinks that I am going to be nice, I'll drop the bomb."	"Being nice, not just as a diversionary tactic, will better service our relationship."
• "I'll get even if it's the last, slyest thing I do."	"One of the last things I can use is bittersweet revenge."
• "I'll show her how mad I am by setting her up and then lowering the boom."	"Better that I show myself and my partner that I want to do well by us."
• "I'll make it so he can't question my intentions, and if he does I'll just say I was only trying to be funny."	"The only person that I fool by thinking hostility has value is myself."
• "I'll get even; and I can always say that I didn't mean anything by it."	"Fooling around with another's mind is a foolhardy thing to do."
• "Hit them right when they least expect it and right where they least expect it - that's my motto."	"When I negatively do the unexpected the only thing I can expect is trouble."

THOUGHTS THAT CAUSE BACKDOOR AGGRESSION *(Cont'd)*	THOUGHT SUBSTITUTES THAT WILL PREVENT BACKDOOR AGGRESSION *(Cont'd)*
• "What a joy to confuse others to the point that they don't know what to think."	"Joy comes from pleasing others, not confusing them."
• "Surprise tactics do more harm and that's exactly what I want to do to get even."	"Surprise tactics do more harm all right, more harm to me, that is."

Dealing with another's hostile tactics in a way that discourages them can be accomplished by applying the following steps:

1. *Don't blame yourself.* Don't conclude that you're bad because another is treating you badly.
2. *Use compassion, not other blame.* See that others' salty conduct reflects their hostilities and insecurities and have compassion for their unfortunate state of mind.
3. *Don't think that you are required to respond to the two-edged comment.* In fact, fully ignoring the comment by physically turning away from the person while not saying anything may be the best tactic. However, if you do decide to comment about his or her caustic comment:
4. *Make prepared positive statements that may discourage such negative chatter in the future.* Such firm, no-nonsense declarations could include:

   • "I'm not sure what you meant by what you just said, but I do know for sure that I didn't like it."
   • "In the future, if you don't have something halfway decent to say, I don't want to hear it. But if you violate my wishes I will not listen."
   • "It's unfair to me to be required to decode your message in order to have a snowball's chance in hell of understanding you."

- "These are the times that try men's souls, but I'll try to understand and accept you in spite of your two-faced hostile comments."
- "It's only fair for me to inform you that I plan on letting your unfair comments go in one ear and out the other."
- "Whatever it is that you're bothering yourself about, I'm going to make it a point not to let it bother me."
- "No matter what you say about me or how you say it, I can still find value to myself."
- "Next time you shoot the works, try not to shoot it in two parts."

Be a good host; don't make yourself hostile and then use backhand compliments as backdoor aggression. There is more than one way to give someone the backhand. The physical backhand will cause physical hurt. Backhanded compliments hurt your chances of love's survival. Such misbehavior will backfire, destroying your relationship by putting it on the constant critical protection alert. Instead, opt for more pleasant contacts by saying what you mean and meaning what you say when you declare your intentions to be up front in a more appealing, harder to resist manner.

Note. From *Head Over Heart in Love: 25 Guides to Rational Passion* by Bill Borcherdt. Copyright © 1996, Professional Resource Exchange, Inc., P.O. Box 15560, Sarasota, FL 34277-1560.

The Cost of Avoiding
Conflict at All Costs

Most things in life and love don't come easy - except trouble. Troublesome times stemming from individual differences in love relationships are no exception. How these differences are approached is what determines their effects on the loving. If approached effectively they can broaden a relationship in that one can learn more from someone who thinks and speaks differently from them - provided they listen to the other. If approached in an ineffective manner these same differences will narrow the love by sending it down the garden path of overreaction. Nothing between any two people is perfect. Between human imperfections and naturally different tastes and preferences of any couple, conflicts will arise. There are three basic manners of dealing with such inevitable occurrences:

1. *Directly.* Forthrightly declaring the obvious and then working from there to resolve the matter (e.g., "The two of us seem to have different opinions on this matter. What do you think of the idea of putting our heads together and brainstorming possible ways to settle the issue?").
2. *Indirectly.* Hinting around nonverbally that you have a concern (e.g., sighing, loudly clearing your throat, excessively raising your eyebrows) or partially exposing your concern with words (e.g., "I suppose you think that just because I'm not yelling there's nothing wrong" or "I'll bet you can't guess what's on my mind"). These are ex-

amples of sneaking up on the difference in a semi-revealing way.
3. *Avoidance at all costs.* Not "rocking the boat" at any cost is a method of tip-toeing around conflicts that pushes the disagreement process underground.

The first communication strategy makes no bones or mistakes about what you are up against by way of incompatibility. The second method of relating may lead to eventually disclosing the facts of your differences. The third mode of handling conflict is the one that may seem the least expensive at first but costs much more later. Burying conflict can lead to the death of a relationship. Dealing with conflict anxiety by pushing the long-range negative consequences of avoidance out of mind in favor of the immediate relief of looking the other way takes its eventual toll on a relationship that is otherwise in good standing. Motivation by present convenience is not a long-range convenience item. Immediate relief is followed by long-range indigestion due to avoidance of conflict realities. The long-run cost of avoiding short-term conflict is as follows:

1. *Creates stockpiling en route to angry restraint.* Keeping your qualms to yourself provides an appearance of peace that often betrays undetected resentment.
2. *Results in eventual expressions of hostility and animosity.* The pressure cooker of angry restraint is always at risk to boiling over so long as fraudulent agreement is promoted on the outside while disagreement is made to steam on the inside.
3. *Encourages mistrust.* When people either say what they think you want to hear or say nothing, it is difficult to know what they really believe or stand for. Whether they tell or don't tell you their position, the nagging doubt of whether they are simply following their proven pattern of avoiding conflict at all costs lingers.
4. *Creates relationship wishy-washyness.* When you don't say what you mean and don't mean what you say, it becomes

difficult to identify what values your relationship stands for. As a result, confusion and drifting weaken your identity.

5. *Promotes falling for anything as a consequence for standing for nothing.* Frightening yourself from declaring your values leaves you open to others' suggestions that may fit for them but may not be right for you. By taking on someone else's values you will likely defend them less staunchly than if they were yours. Often this represents a roundabout way of conflict avoidance.

6. *Accelerates fear of the unknown.* Viewing the unknown that follows direct confrontation as being bigger than life prevents you from experiencing it and then becoming simply a part of life. Exposure to a fear tends to weaken it; avoidance has a strengthening effect.

7. *Encourages increased hypersensitivity.* Walking on the thin ice of conflict avoidance encourages a prickly way of relating that is an outcome of not knowing where you stand with the person of unknown values.

8. *Creates a potential market for guilt and shame.* Errors of omission, like errors of commission, are often followed by self-blame. Dishonesty as a result of pretending not to know what you do know is often made to create these down-on-yourself emotions.

9. *Does not solve problems.* The most obvious handicap of leaving unsaid what is a concern for you is that problems go unattended while they further erode your relationship.

10. *Diminishes mutual respect.* You may not like it when your loved one levels with you, but you may be more likely to respect his or her honest efforts to call a spade a spade in hopes of contributing to meeting and beating your differences head-on.

11. *Clogs rather than clears up the airways.* When done in a civilized, unangry manner, going into the teeth of your conflicts while trying not to eat each other alive can provide much emotional slack. Playing "let's pretend we

agree on everything" leaves a heavy cloud of stress and strain to reckon with.

The only two ways to never have a conflict with your loved one are to never value anything or have a partner who is a clone of your values. Both are unlikely possibilities! To always go with the flow or to never think for yourself rather than being aboveboard in trying to come to terms with your individual differences can be a costly style of relating. The charge for such avoidances is too high to not take charge of addressing differences of concern that are a natural part of life and love in a less-avoident, less costly way.

•

Note. From *Head Over Heart in Love: 25 Guides to Rational Passion* by Bill Borcherdt. Copyright © 1996, Professional Resource Exchange, Inc., P.O. Box 15560, Sarasota, FL 34277-1560.

The One and Only
Love Syndrome:
Hazards of Putting All
Your Eggs in One Basket

"They seem like two peas in a pod." "They are made out of the same mold." "I can't imagine them doing something or going someplace without each other." "Here they come - the inseparables." People who make one another's company an almost always exclusive outing will often find these references of admiration directed their way. Like a lot of lofty ideals, this "two as one" picture-perfect portrait appears as good as gold, but soon becomes tarnished when its realities are exposed. Exclusive, one-and-only-one-true-love notions are not the only way to structure a love relationship and may well be far from the best method. To completely cast your lot with another is to ask for the troubles of unhealthy pressure and fear. After all, if you are the one and only life's and love's blood for me, does that not put you, as the strong one, to forever and always meet my emotional and compatability expectations - without which I will emotionally die on the vine? To sense that someone has defined his or her requirements of life and love and then has further concluded that you are the only person in the whole wide world who can sponsor them leads to ultraresponsible thoughts and feelings in you that are akin to living in a pressure cooker. This arrangement also puts the dependent weaker mate on constant hyperalertness, worrying about whether your partner's next step toward you will be the last. Feelings of desperation and controlling behaviors are likely to follow such fearfulness.

Statements such as "I REALLY need you and only you," "I could never make it without you," "You're all I ever wanted and I am nothing without you," "PLEASE don't ever leave me, I could never survive alone," and "Let's do everything together" may be good soap-opera material but have no place in a relationship that has hopes for mutual emotional balance. Both the sender and receiver of such life-or-death devotions suffer. Efforts to fuse, to give up the search for your values by meshing with someone else, puts undue tension on all concerned, leaving a void where it would be better had individual differences been allowed to flourish. Specific disadvantages of all-or-nothing relationship thinking include:

1. *Self-interest is lost.* It would be better for both if they would put themselves first and their partner a close second, rather than their partner first and themselves a distant second.

2. *Builds anger and resentment.* Not sorting out the difference between sharing your life with someone and sacrificing your life for someone will likely eventually create anger and resentment while trying to be all things for another person.

3. *Prevents self-discovery and personality well-roundedness.* Trapping yourself in a routine that has you continually looking to another results in limited exposure to your options in life.

4. *Familiarity breeds contempt.* Short of resentment and direct argument is impatience, curtness, and becoming quickly annoyed. These prickly aggravations often reflect being around someone too much.

5. *Appreciation for novelty is lost.* Novelty helps make life interesting. Demands for everlasting security that are sought from an unchanging, unbalanced relationship kill novel possibilities.

6. *Chronic discord.* The more opportunity people have to have their differences be rubbed the wrong way, the more of a pattern such differences are likely to become.

7. *Often an abrupt splitting from the relationship.* Suffocated by the demands for exclusiveness by the dependent, weaker party, the stronger mate is often apt to abruptly exit rather than continue to expose himself or herself to such clinging behaviors.

What follows is a list of irrational, compulsive self-sentences that reflect harmful, exclusive dependence on a loved one. Each is matched with a rational statement, freer of thought and emotion, that reflects more *inter*dependent striving.

IRRATIONAL, SUFFOCATING IDEA	RATIONAL, LIBERATING COUNTER
• "I could never get along without my partner and therefore I need him to be at my beck and call."	"I love my partner very much, but I did spend all my time without him before we met, so I can spend time apart now too."
• "I can't afford to be at anything but an arm's length from my mate, because I just couldn't take it emotionally."	"I can ill afford to not spend time away from my partner because if I don't find my own way I'll make myself forever dependent on her - and that wouldn't be fair to either one of us."
• "I need my partner to structure my time and to entertain me because I'm not very creative that way."	"The ability to entertain oneself, by oneself, is a central ingredient of mental health; better that I use a fair portion of my time to work on my mental health."
• "If I don't make it dramatically clear that I want to spend most of my waking hours with my loved one, she might think that I'm losing love for her."	"Overkill kills love! Pouring it on thick as to how I want to spend almost all my time with my partner is not necessary to document my love for her, and I can only hope that she is mature enough to understand this."

IRRATIONAL, SUFFOCATING IDEA *(Cont'd)*	RATIONAL, LIBERATING COUNTER *(Cont'd)*
• "I must devote all the time of my life to my mate and I can't stand it when I'm not able to do so."	"Where is it written that I absolutely must cover the time of our relationship like a blanket?"
• "If I don't bird-dog our time together I might lose my loved one to someone else."	"Sticking to our relationship like flypaper will likely end up with me tracking it to death. Besides, if I lose my partner to someone else, he loses me too!"

Consider these countering ideas and their value to contributing to making your love relationship into a variety show rather than an exclusive showing. Give your relationship some emotional slack by not relying on it to provide all that you hope to gain in life. Consider the following advantages of taking a more well-rounded view of your love life; advantages that you can ill afford to go without. To gain them, go without contact in your relationship for temporary periods of time.

1. *Helps you learn more from each other.* Things discovered while apart can be fodder for discussion when together and will allow you to learn from someone who has done something that you haven't.
2. *Helps you learn more about yourself.* When you do things on your own you learn a lot about yourself - your likes and dislikes, strengths, and weaknesses.
3. *Helps you learn more about the other.* When your mate treads water alone, you find out more about him or her from his or her finding out more about himself or herself.
4. *Demonstrates a decent respect for and an appreciation of individual differences.* More fully understanding and accepting that your partner may not want to spend his or her time the way you want to breeds mutual acceptance of the type found in relationships that favorably develop.

5. *Adds stimulation.* Outside entry leads to inside relationship arousal and the excitement that comes from newness.

6. *Cancels out possessive and jealous tendencies.* The best way to change an irrational belief is to act against it. Allowing for time apart conditions a safer and more emotionally secure way of believing in yourself and your relationship.

7. *Decreases demandingness.* Rotation and balance by way of time structuring is a permissive, nondemanding way to account for your relationship time.

8. *Provides a vote of confidence.* Learning to be comfortable while apart implies a vote of confidence in self, other, and the relationship due to your belief in all three being able to handle such absence.

9. *Moves from a selfish to a self-interested stance.* Showing an interest in your partner, not only for the amount of time he or she can provide for you, but also the amount he or she can give to himself or herself deflates "me, me, and only me" tendencies.

10. *Means less worry about the often ultimate separation fear - death.* Demonstrating the capacity for personal enjoyment while living with your mate can help to combat worry about what you will do in the event of his or her death before you; consequently, you make room for enjoying the time you have alive together.

11. *Means less quantity, more quality.* Absence can make the heart grow fonder. Enrichment of living replaces marking love's time by weaving in *and* out of your mate's life.

12. *Aids self-confidence - not just love confidence.* Being confident that you can make it through the night with your loved one's presence is called love confidence. Knowing that you can emotionally manage without your mate is a fuller form of self-sufficiency, called self-confidence.

13. *Moves from dependence while avoiding the opposite extreme, independence, to the more well-balanced approach of interdependence.* In doing so, added perspective is attained and emotional well-being is added to the relationship.

14. *Contributes to a broader worldview.* Permitting yourself a broader exposure to life under the umbrella of your own resources demonstrates that you can safely experience and better understand where you fit in the overall scheme of things.

Afford your love life the advantages of taking on more loving interests yourself while encouraging your partner to do the same. Requesting or providing a total devotion of time and energy is a dead end. Such a no-win arrangement places you and yours in an emotional pressure cooker that will get you steamed. Putting all your marbles in one pot will make it more likely that you will lose them - in more ways than one! Shoot for the golden balanced mean instead of declaring a one-and-only golden rule for love. That way you will more likely rule out the hazards of destructive emotional fall-out and rule in helpings of personal and interpersonal well-being.

Note. From *Head Over Heart in Love: 25 Guides to Rational Passion* by Bill Borcherdt. Copyright © 1996, Professional Resource Exchange, Inc., P.O. Box 15560, Sarasota, FL 34277-1560.

Give a Little, Gain a Lot: Proposing Workable Compromises

Finding a way to resolve individual differences is no easy task. When two people want different things but only one can be gained, methods of getting past such stand-offs had best be created. Without methods of conflict resolution, the relationship stays stuck in its differences, unable to go forward toward higher-order goals. No one gains in such a stalemate. Moving off the center of one's differences can be accomplished through a combination of compromising attitude adjustments followed by compromising behavioral proposals. What is suggested as an alternative might not be exactly what I had hoped to gain, nor specifically what you were looking to garner, but a happier medium option that we can both better live with. This is the essence of a workable compromise; it works for *both* of us to a reasonable degree. One of us doesn't get a few crumbs and the other the majority of the loaf, but each gets a part of the loaf so that the hunger pains of our wants and desires are satisfied to a reasonable degree. It's similar to purchasing a car, where buyer and seller walk away from the sale each believing that they got their money's worth. Each may even believe that they got slightly more than their money's worth, but not too much more.

Gaining a lot by giving a little may sound contradictory. This is because we are accustomed to believing that to gain a lot one is required to hang on tightly to what one has plus energetically seek more of it. To not assertively strive for goals seems to indicate lack of ambition. In creating workable compromises it is helpful to take a long-range view of life. If I have a bead on the same goal that my partner has - for instance, where we are going to eat out, how one of the children is to be disciplined, or who can keep some money left over after paying the bills for spending - a good question to ask myself would be, "Do I want to wholeheartedly pursue my desires and feel good right now in doing so, or do I want to feel better later on from reaping the benefits of putting my mate in a kinder, gentler mood by meeting him or her halfway?" Seeing beyond one's nose by appreciating the long-term advantages of compromising activities is the first step in the direction of give-and-take. Until that profitable light at the end of the compromising tunnel is turned on, it is unlikely one will be turned on to a happier medium.

What advantages can be gained from giving a little? Well, make a proposal and find out! Best that you come to these proposals with attitudes such as:

- "Compromising will be to my mate's *and* to my advantage" rather than, "I have to see there is a lot for me in my offer before I make it."
- "If my partner is happier with the compromise, then I will be too" rather than, "The only way I can be happy is to have my own way."
- "By compromising I can work on my tolerance for not getting fully what I want" rather than, "I can't stand it when I don't get what I need, especially when I'm deserving of it."
- "Compromising is definitely in my best interest because it encourages my partner to be more fun to be around" rather than, "When I compromise I lose, and I hate losing."
- "When I lose by compromising I win by way of goodwill" rather than, "What is lost by compromise is lost and cannot be made up for in any other way."

- "Argumentation, demanding that I have my own way, puts a real strain on my love life" rather than, "If I don't look out for myself by straining myself to insist that I get exactly what I want, nobody else will."
- "Meet someplace in between rather than try to beat your differences to death" rather than, "Beat the other person to the punch or you'll lose everything."
- "Care less about getting my own way and I will be better off" rather than, "If you win out you will be a better person."
- "Both of us will get more bees and benefits with honey" rather than, "Go for broke until you break the will of the other."

Suggested questions and statements that can introduce compromising possibilities include:

- "The idea of _____ is different than what you or I are proposing; what do you think of it?"
- "What do you think of the two of us sitting down and putting our heads together and see how many other possibilities we can brainstorm?"
- "I wonder what are our other possibilities - got any suggestions?"
- "What might be some brighter and better options than those we have already thought about?"
- "Would you be willing to consider other ways of looking at things than those we have already suggested?"
- "Would you be willing to consider an option that neither of us has proposed, but might be something we could both better live with?"
- "Rather than arguing our differences out, what do you think of settling on happier medium compromises?"
- "Can we agree that neither of us is 100% right and work toward possible solutions that we have not yet considered acceptable?"
- "What do you think of the idea of each of us giving a little on the chance we will meet someplace in between?"

- "In your opinion, what do you think it would take for us to find a common ground?"
- "What do you think would happen if we decided to switch rather than fight?"

Structuring your compromising message in such civilized terms makes possible the following advantages:

1. *Deflates resentment.* "You" questions signal that another's opinions are important. It's difficult to resent someone under such flattering terms.
2. *Opens up the floodgates of other possibilities.* Serious problem solving begins, whereby both parties go from opposite sides of the table and fighting each other to the same side of the table to fight the problem.
3. *Makes you and your position harder to resist.* It's more difficult to disagree with someone who asks you what to think, rather than telling you how to think.
4. *Prevents jawboning.* It's difficult to argue with someone who is considering possibilities other than those proposed.
5. *Eases tension.* Tensionless living is created by taking the wind out of disagreement's sails by actively seeking options of agreement.
6. *Makes for better connections in the future.* It is easier to be or get in touch with one who comes to encounters with you in the spirit of cooperation and compromise.
7. *Signals hope.* There is always hope for resolving differences and relationships prevailing when associating with someone who is not shy about being willing to bend.
8. *Unleashes creativity.* Agreeing to disagree, yet finding portions of agreement, sets the stage for creating new ways of looking at old differences.
9. *Promotes general goodwill.* Good compromises, meaning those that benefit both parties, leave a lingering sense of interpersonal well-being.
10. *Contributes to your own mental health, especially increased tolerance.* Increased emotional well-being is gained from

making yourself ready and willing to meet someone half-way.

Granted, with some differences of vital interests there can be no compromises. However, such dig-in-your-heels strongholds are held to more frequently than is necessary. Proposals made in the spirit of compromise can save a lot of emotional and relationship wear and tear. Giving a little can result in gaining a lot, again and again, and again.

Note. From *Head Over Heart in Love: 25 Guides to Rational Passion* by Bill Borcherdt. Copyright © 1996, Professional Resource Exchange, Inc., P.O. Box 15560, Sarasota, FL 34277-1560.

Love's Refusals:
More Gracefully Taking and
Giving No for an Answer

One of the best indicators of the strength of a love relationship is for each partner to feel comfortable in exercising their right of refusing the other's request. Due to individual differences in matters of tastes and preferences, relationships that aren't able to stand the test of accepting refusal - without resentment - are unlikely to stand the test of time. "No" can be a love word in that such limit setting promotes a relationship philosophy of "I value our relationship too much to not set boundaries on how far and often I am willing to extend myself on its behalf." Such a thumbs-down response to a request for time, service, or entertainment sharing further implies, "If I consistently go against my better judgment by agreeing to do things that I would not be happy in doing, I will likely end up feeling irritation toward you, me, and us. Compliance at all costs to personal happiness is too expensive a risk."

Learning how to take and give no for an answer is a method that can build emotional stamina into a relationship, allowing it to surpass original agreement-by-compulsion limitations. To appreciate the advantages of nondefensively sending and gracefully receiving no for an answer can help free you up for such honest communication. These benefits will now be identified.

1. *Conveys a vote of confidence in you by your partner.* Turning down another's request implies that the other believes you are secure enough to not disturb yourself about a rejection of your request.
2. *Helps establish openness and honesty as a method of communication.* Direct means of communicating compliance or noncompliance with another's requests helps to break down barriers to conversation. Knowing that tip-toeing around your mate's request or your refusal of it is not necessary is a refreshing slant to increasing compatibility.
3. *Less resentment build-up.* Being true to yourself in giving no for an answer while tolerantly accepting no when the shoe is on the other foot dissolves feelings of resentment before they get off the ground.
4. *Helps keep the relationship freshened.* A breath of fresh air enters the relationship upon removing caution flags that represent fraudulent agreements on the one hand and hidden angry compliance on the other.
5. *Establishes a nondefensive basis for the relationship.* Not feeling required by your relationship to sheepishly overexplain your request or refusal puts partners in a more harmonious, less worrisome mood.
6. *Strikes at the heart of disapproval anxiety.* Relationships that live their life by the approval principle - "I must always have the approval of significant others," - often don't live very long nor very satisfyingly. Giving no for an answer helps to put a dent in the tendency to sabotage a relationship by overextending yourself for it in search of total approval.
7. *Makes more efficient use of relationship time.* Valuable time is lost in the process of tip-toeing around or apologetically explaining your request or your refusal of another's request.
8. *Lessens self and other doubts.* Confidence in your ability to more gracefully take and give no for an answer helps to lessen second thoughts about yourself in relationship to your mate.

9. *Feeds into general characteristics of emotional well-being.*
Learning not to take another's refusal personally, discovering how to get yourself past your fears and insecurities about refusing someone else's request, and finding out the value of not thinking you are on trial and therefore must defensively explain yourself when giving no for an answer are all valuable contributions to your mental health.

10. *Allows you to practice a more helpful and healthful way of thinking.*

IRRATIONAL THOUGHTS TO BE DECREASED	RATIONAL THOUGHTS TO BE INCREASED
• "If I refuse my partner's requests he might think that I don't love him - and that would be awful."	"It is important for both of us to learn that love and obligation are not the same - the fact that one of us might not understand this at a given point in time is not the end of the world."
• "I owe my partner favorable consideration of her request and when I refuse her asking I should feel guilty for not holding up to my part of the deal."	"I owe it to our relationship to fairly consider my mate's requests, and when I give them unfavorable consideration I need not consider myself to be an evil, villainous person."
• "Especially because my partner almost always says yes to my requests, I in turn have to almost always honor his wants."	"Even though my partner is notably consistent in responding yes to my wants, there is no golden rule that says I must always do unto others as they most always do for and unto me."
• "If I practically always agree to do what my partner asks of me, she must practically always comply with what I request of her."	"My version of the reverse golden rule - others should do unto me as I do unto them - does not exist, and to try to enforce such a myth can only bring me and my relationship a lot of trouble."

IRRATIONAL THOUGHTS TO BE DECREASED *(Cont'd)*	RATIONAL THOUGHTS TO BE INCREASED *(Cont'd)*
• "Whenever my mate refuses my request, it will be a good long time before I honor his again."	"Better that I maturely accept my partner's right to refuse my request rather than childishly protest against this reality."

The message of more gracefully taking and giving no for an answer is not that *sometimes* doing things to accommodate a relationship - even when you don't feel up to it - is not in order and doesn't have a life of its own in more peacefully extending it. Rather, more to the point is that to do so in a steady manner will likely backfire in the long run. More tolerantly and acceptingly taking no and giving no for an answer will supply some of the give-and-take necessary to strengthen the confidence in the you, me, and us parts of your love life. You make yourself feel strong enough not to feel guilty in your refusals, your partner feels secure enough to not take your refusal personally, and both of you wisely decide not to hold the content of each other's requests and responses against one another. Building such relationship and emotional endurance will help to more gracefully and peaceably endure the ebb and flow, give-and-take, vital balance between oftentimes honoring but sometimes refusing your loved one's requests.

Note. From *Head Over Heart in Love: 25 Guides to Rational Passion* by Bill Borcherdt. Copyright © 1996, Professional Resource Exchange, Inc., P.O. Box 15560, Sarasota, FL 34277-1560.

Love Is Blind -
Including Self-Love

"Those who love themselves have no rivals." In spite of the preceding statement, love of self is often affirmed as the gateway to emotional well-being. Commercialized suggestions to love or at least like yourself and that you have to love yourself before you can love others have the following often-overlooked side effects.

1. *Overfocus and self-indulgence.* Concentration on the self-love task at hand limits your ability to occupy life with others due to preoccupation with self.
2. *Ego overtones.* Loving of self often means proving oneself. Such a form of self-measurement can easily be a never-ending process.
3. *Paradoxical social effects.* The more that you make yourself hung up on yourself, the less energy you will have to invest in your social group.
4. *Loss of a broader vital purpose.* Not being able to get beyond your own navel will leave you without more varied meaning to your life. A sense of accomplishment will be lost if your main accomplishment is self-love.
5. *All-consuming.* Those who try to prove the self by loving themselves will spend most of their time trying to fill up their bottomless pit of self-consumption.
6. *Encourages wonderfulizing and Pollyannaism.* Thinking that (self-) love is the answer to everything invites a worldview that is laid-back to a fault - assuming that every-

thing will automatically turn out for the better. Such over-looking of the negative realities of life leaves one ill-equipped to cope with them.

7. *Temptations of self-deification.* Self-involvement conven-iences a holier-than-thou mentality. Continually focus-ing on self is less than a hop, skip, or jump away from arrogantly concluding that you are better than others.

8. *Loss of social group camaraderie.* Finding your self-love revelations difficult to stomach, your associates are likely to abandon your company in the service of more pleas-urable pursuits. After all, who likes to be around a love-struck person?

Falling head over heels in love with yourself will prevent you from seeing up to and beyond your own nose. Instead of loving yourself, try accepting yourself. Self-acceptance principles provide a purer path to emotional well-being in that they set aside self-rating by the external standards that self-love employs. Getting yourself strung out on me, me, and only me limits your vision and discourages others from approaching you. Instead of letting yourself be blinded by self-love, see that such disadvantage will get you no place - fast. Then, opt for self-acceptance principles and their broader, more self- *and* other-enlightened view. This will likely help you to feel better while staying on the better side of your so-cial group.

Note. From *Head Over Heart in Love: 25 Guides to Rational Passion* by Bill Borcherdt. Copyright © 1996, Professional Resource Exchange, Inc., P.O. Box 15560, Sarasota, FL 34277-1560.

Opposites Attract - and Attack:
And Twenty-Nine Other
Paradoxes of Dating and Mating

What seemed novel, exciting, and compatible while court-ing in a relationship often appears prickly and downright aggravating as it unfolds. During the honeymoon phase, personality traits of loved ones seem to accommodate one's tastes; during this post-rosy era these same characteristics are often viewed as disruptive. Drinking *to* your lover for his or her entertaining features is replaced with drinking *because* of them as the relationship wear and tear pushes on. Why is it that what attracted you to your partner at first blush is the very thing that you complain about and attack later in the game? It is likely that somewhere between the first and the ninth inning, beliefs about what your partner's unique traits mean for you are made to change. It is this altered way of thinking with more than a little help from your low frustra-tion tolerance that results in a beginning good thing going full circle into a bad thing.

Newness wears thin when what was discovered in some-one else is in strong contrast to your value preferences. Al-though stimulating and attractive at first, what started as an exciting possibility will end as a buried, flash-in-the-pan op-portunity unless tolerance and acceptance levels are made to match your beginning enthusiasm. Exposure to what is found to be attractive often turns out to be the deathbed of love. Love and glamour eventually waning is a paradox and can be explained in the following tinseled ideas contrasted with pessimistic notions that reflect an overreaction to the real world of individual differences.

BEGINNING SELF-STATEMENTS OF ATTRACTION	LATER SELF-STATEMENTS OF DETRACTION
• "How exciting to meet someone so different from me."	"I can't stand such contrary behavior."
• "I've never met anyone so different - I just know that I will always feel so interested in him."	"He is so different it's sickening."
• "She is just perfect for me because she fills in all my missing personality parts."	"How could I ever fall for someone so different than me I'll never know!"
• "I've never felt so excited in my life - I just know that this feeling will last forever."	"Another minute with this creep and I'll die."
• "How can something that feels so good ever turn out to be something bad?"	"How this relationship ever had some good in it is beyond me."
• "How fascinating to find someone so far apart from my manner. I just know I will be able to change some of those differences in him to accommodate my manner."	"Trying to change someone who is as stupid as he is really gets to me."
• "She needs somebody quite different to show her the way to salvation."	"She needs a good kick in the ass to find the road to salvation."
• "How absolutely superb to be around someone so different from me."	"No one should have to put up with someone like him - he is different all right!"

Decisions! Decisions! Resolving this dilemma of love at the beginning and hate at the end can be done by choosing from the basic options available. When repeated exposure to the reality of individual differences kills the dream of unending excitement of those same differences you can (a) work on your courage to leave what you have determined to be irreconcilable differences, (b) try like hell to use the relationship to improve your mental health by heightening your tolerance levels for these differences by making it a point to not whine and scream about them, or (c) try to negotiate compromise and trade-offs with your partner that will expect each of you to try harder to please the other while not being so hard to please.

Other paradoxes of dating and mating include:

1. *Exercise, yet give up freedom of choice.* As Sartre the philosopher points out, partners often ask each other to give of their love freely - but once given, to give up the option of ever changing their mind.
2. *Live for the present and future but focus on the past.* Opening up old wounds about past depreciations is often the order of the day, while starting over with a new, appreciative beginning is given feeble lip service.
3. *Close and secure, yet distant and fearful.* Couples look for emotional security in their attachment but often feel distant and fearful about the possibility of not gaining a return attachment. Such emotionally dependent leanings defeat the original comforts and advantages of joining forces.
4. *Good intentions of pooling resources but with poor scorekeeping methods.* Tabulating who is contributing more and who less loses sight of the original intended advantage that "two heads are better than one." As long as the sum total of combined efforts adds up to maximum performance, why contaminate this advantage with an itemization of efforts?
5. *Wish to communicate their views - after the other is informed what theirs is!* "Let me tell you my side of the story - so I

can enlighten you as to what yours is and where you went wrong" illustrates the double messages that communicators often give. Attending more to understanding others rather than getting them to understand you, or resisting the temptation to put words in other people's mouths as to their understanding, can remedy the false idea that "I know better than you do about you."

6. *Wishing to trust the other without first trusting self.* This paradox will dissolve when you trust yourself to be able to get through the night preferably with, but also without, the apple of your eye. Believing in your own self-reliance affords you the ability of trusting the other. Such refreshing independence can depressurize relationship stress.

7. *Seek personal and relationship responsibility but chronically pass the buck.* Many want to further their development, but few are willing to pay the price for responsible self-living. Finger pointing in an effort to make the other responsible for one's problems and upsets is the rule rather than the exception. "You make me mad" had best be replaced with, "I upset myself about my partner's manner and conduct; now how can I work hard to upset myself less?" Such an attitude will demolish this other-blaming irony.

8. *Want to get to know each other - without asking.* Although it seems easier to establish your knowledge of another by mind reading, such guesswork provides another example of how it isn't easy to take the easy way out. It may be a little more work to prompt another's opinion than to assume you know, but such direct tracking is worth the effort. Understanding based on chance rather than fact is likely to set in motion a chain of misunderstandings.

9. *Desire to express love, yet try to instill hurt.* Dramatizing your partner's flaws and sore spots is often a calculated effort to induce the other to feel hurt. Hitting below the belt is a pale effort to perfume your own hurt that came from taking something your mate said or did personally.

10. *Want to be understanding - but not at the expense of being understood.* Self-centeredness blocks desires to offer understanding. Unconditional understanding, with no strings attached, rather than "I'll understand you if you make it a point to understand me (and you go first)," will make for fewer walls and more bridges in your relationships.

11. *Insist they not be used but have provisions as a relationship foundation.* Many find it difficult to accept that they don't stay in a love relationship for the health of it. Not using one another is not a sacred item. On the contrary, people date and mate, and have market value to one another, because they are able to use each other's assets (e.g., humor, looks, creativity, problem-solving abilities) to enrich their own life. The ideal relationship is being able to use one another's provision as a pleasant rather than as a demeaning reality, as it is often pictured to be.

12. *Overlooking contributions for the other as promoting self-interest.* Doing favors for your partner is really doing favors for yourself. Making it convenient for your mate to be happy by accommodating his or her wishes will improve the quality of your life in that the other will likely be more fun to be around.

13. *Love running on fear and demand.* Madly loving another out of fear of losing that person and as a demand for a return on your efforts will wear thin. "I'll fuse with you and treat you so exceptionally nice that you couldn't possibly not love me in return" represents love turned frantic.

14. *Start by making self hard to resist and end to the contrary.* The trick of encouraging another to care and to stay caring about you is to put your better foot forward and keep it there. Keeping up the beat of appreciations to the neglect of depreciations is an ongoing task that few are up for. A philosophy of complacency rather than sustained effort is often permitted to rule the roost.

15. *Wish lists as good, demand lists as bad.* Wanting advantages from your relationship is a good thing. Such wishes

provide meaning to your togetherness. Finding the tolerance to prevent blowing up these preferences into demands is perhaps the primary ingredient of a satisfying love relationship. "I want certain pleasures from you - therefore you have to make these pleasant provisions" had best be replaced with, "I certainly want definite favors from you, but I don't require them, and whether or not you extend them is fully up to you."

16. *Asking when you are really telling.* "I would like to hear what you have to say on the matter, as long as it doesn't interfere with what I have already decided" is often a statement that is a sure-fire way of pulling the rug out from under any hopes for two-way communication. Communication is cut off by asking and answering a question too thoroughly. Rather, as Will Rogers suggests, better to leave a doubt to hang a conversation on.

17. *Love addiction as bad, need as allegedly good.* Who's kidding whom? Don't let the experts pull the wool over your eyes with this applesauced brand of double-think. Much to-do is being made about love addiction as bad - rightly so. But what is an addiction? Answer: a need. So what are most experts telling their clients? Answer: That they have needs for love. Talk about talking out of both sides of one's mouth! Just as it wouldn't be advisable to tell an alcoholic he needed alcohol, neither would it be wise to inform someone who has inclinations toward love dependency that they need love! Resolve this paradox by seeing that love, as great as it might be, isn't a necessity.

18. *Fusion and confusion of love and dependency.* Sane love is being able to get close to someone and being able to let go if it is in your best interest to do so. Need is attaching yourself to someone but not being able to let go out of fear of discomfort. The paradox is that the tighter you dependently cling to the one you love, the more likely you will put pressure on the relationship, defeating its loving purposes.

19. *Love provides stability and allows control over your life, yet fate has you by the hair.* These two contrasting ideas result

in becoming emotionally seasick. On the one hand, love is viewed as the answer to everything; on the other hand, it is seen as a dangerous venture that will do you in if you fail.

20. *Prioritize negotiating, yet slam the door and walk out.* What you know is not as significant as what you do with what you know. Most people emphasize the value of open, honest discussion of differences, but when it comes right down to it they will often head for the nearest exit sign, letting the door slam on their behind on their abrupt way out. Be willing to hang around and face the not-too-pleasant music of your differences in the hope of ironing them out.

21. *Acknowledging the art of being wise as knowing what to over-look, yet nitpicking.* In casual discussion most partners will agree to the value of overlooking the other's flaws. However, in the heat of conflict, standing up for the relationship by looking the other way is left by the wayside.

22. *Easy and simple, yet hard and complicated.* Twirling a baton or eating with chopsticks seems easy too - until you try it. Simple doesn't mean simply lived. Partners quickly discover that nothing between humans, no matter how attracted to one another, is perfect. The trick is to accept rather than overreact to inevitable relationship complications.

23. *If the love is good, the sex will naturally follow.* Sex is natural but not necessarily naturally easy. Although they are often not quick to admit it, couples find that love can be an interference to and a distraction from sex. Focusing on how much you love the living doll or big brute rather than sexual ideation will not create sexual arousal. It's best to understand and accept the less-than-ideal reality that love and sex don't go together like a horse and carriage. Flooding your mind with specialized sexual fantasies can be a solution to this practical problem.

24. *Proclaimed exclusiveness, yet pronounced other-person interest.* Shortly into a relationship, the one and only theory

is replaced by nonmonogamous reality desires. "Thou shalt have no other love and sex inclinations other than for me" is another golden rule that tarnishes in the light of everyday living. The longer you date and mate the more likely that you will have desires for others. This is to combat the monotony of sameness and because no one person is likely to provide all of what you find endearing in a mate.

25. *Love as earned rather than given freely.* Many of the best things in life may be free, but love is likely to better stand the test of time when it is earned. Elbow grease as helping to maintain the conditions of the relationship promotes give-and-take and discourages the take-for-grantedness that is often allowed to set in.

26. *Total honesty but leaving room for creative hypocrisy.* White lies had best be set apart from black truths in the service of relationship upkeep. Having a love affair with never-ending honesty is one sure way of disrupting a good thing. If it is discovered that your mate doesn't take some truths in stride, accommodating rather than challenging their sore spots had best be considered.

27. *Dependence and independence as extremes, interdependence as ideal.* Between suffocating one another and passing each other like ships in the night is the rotation and balance, give-and-take pendulum out of which more balanced relationships are made. Like all dating and mating paradoxes, experience well into the relationship is required to arrive at a reasonably happy medium.

28. *Want to extend the relationship, but not at the expense of being right.* When ego pride dictates that being right is sacred, you will likely see your love life die with its rights on. Better that you find and genuinely express some truth to your mate's otherwise contrary position. Try to show more interest in highlighting the accuracy in your partner's ideas than in the nobility of your own.

29. *Provide leeway, but no blank checks.* Leaving your partner room to be himself or herself without hassle is impor-

tant. Yet, putting your two cents in the direction you would like the relationship to go will discourage take-for-grantedness and one-sidedness which has you responding to the other without consideration of your wants. If you give with no expectation in return, you will likely get what you expect. Coming up empty-handed makes it difficult to sustain the energy out of which successful long-term relationships are made.

With this background of paradoxes to contend with, it is little wonder that what began as a match seemingly made in heaven was transposed to a mismatch made in hell. Like any experience, enjoy the excitements of dating and mating as long as you can. Then, get behind yourself and push in understanding, accepting, and unwhiningly coping with these distinctions. Challenge yourself to see if instead of attracting and attacking you cannot attract, remain attracted - and remain attached.

Note. From *Head Over Heart in Love: 25 Guides to Rational Passion* by Bill Borcherdt. Copyright © 1996, Professional Resource Exchange, Inc., P.O. Box 15560, Sarasota, FL 34277-1560.

Servicing Compatibility
By Doing What
Comes *Un*naturally

Humans find it easy to go in the direction they are headed. Doing what comes naturally is fine when one has the luxury of considering only one's own wishes and wants. Doing what comes naturally is naturally easy, but it can put a strain on love relationships. People are different. Differences tend to rub on each other and, unless properly managed, such nudgings can result in lovers disservicing their compatibility goals. Given often-present individual differences, doing what is unnatural can be called upon so as to arrive at a more ac-commodating state. For example, if you have natural ten-dencies to anger yourself when frustrated, you had best un-naturally restrain yourself from such self-directed inclinations. Or, if you find it convenient to sulk, whine, or feel sorry for yourself when you don't get your way, it would be to your advantage to not give expression to such relationship-defeating actions. It can be hard to take the easy way out when encouraging yourself to give vent to natural childish attitude and behavioral tendencies. This is so because of the detrimental relationship and emotional fall-out that is often a consequence of such infantile expressions. Better to unnatu-rally hold back on dishing out such animosities.

Committing *un*natural acts in order to gain fuller com-patibility may seem like an unbecoming expedition for such a harmonious goal. This chapter will explain why conduct that goes against nature is often called for to console individual differences, provide examples of opposing personality forces to be better accommodated, and show how a tolerant, accepting manner of thought lies at the base of more favorable blending-together strivings. Individuals have certain tendencies of temperament as part of their nature: talkative or quiet, humorous or serious, social or private, energetic or low-keyed, adventuresome or cautious. These are just a few. Furthermore, people have differing tastes and approaches to common dimensions in life, such as money management, parenting, projects and special interests, relationships with extended families, religious preferences, love-making methods, and communication styles. Incompatible trait possibilities are almost too numerous to mention! However, all does not have to be lost - if those involved play their cards right.

It is not as easy to swim upstream against the current as it is to swim downstream with it. Yet, that is what is often required by way of pushing oneself to do what is compatible rather than what competes with one's partner. For instance:

- If your partner is a spendthrift and money burns a hole in your pocket, you would do well to unnaturally keep the checkbook balanced rather than spending money sooner than it can be earned.
- If one partner is a firm believer in permissive childrearing while the other is a staunch advocate of strict discipline, rather than scream at each other about their natural differences, it would be to their advantage to unnaturally opt for compromises that bend without breaking.
- If partner number one is gung-ho regarding the advisability of open communication and partner number two is more of a contemplator than a communicator, each would do well to unnaturally push themselves in the direction of the other's preferences in the hope of greeting each other together someplace in between.
- If one party is a social animal and the other has more private yearnings, a word to the wise would be sufficient with

the socialite dimming his or her ambitions and the private member stepping up interest in others - each in the service of more rotation and balance in getting along better.

- The partner with world travel inclinations and the mate more naturally inclined to stay closer to home would do best to develop a philosophy of effort in unnaturally getting behind themselves and pushing themselves toward the other's preferences so as to better accommodate their relationship.

- If one partner is by nature inclined to be physically affectionate to the degree that their mate is so disinclined, it would be better if each would unnaturally take more of a hands-off or hands-on approach, depending on what side of the physical-contact fence each is on.

- If one mate humorously cracks up at the drop of a hat and the other won't laugh for fear his or her face will crack, they would do best if they creatively went against their grain and established more personality well-roundedness in either a lighter or more solemn vein, as the case might be.

- If one person in a relationship adores a spic-and-span domestic look and the other would be happier in a more informal home environment, both partners would do better to give a little, in spite of the fact that such a compromise would be out of character for them.

You might ask yourself, "But what's in it for me? If I venture out of character to willingly and unangrily conform to the happier medium requirements of my love relationship, what do I get out of it?" Humans tend to be creatures of habit, and until they see damned good reasons to moderate their personality preferences, they are unlikely to do so. A naturally right-handed person has little reason to strengthen his weaker left hand until he breaks his dominant hand. Unfortunately, most don't consider bridging compatibility gaps by way of unnatural offerings of compromise until the relationship is about to be severed. However, you can be one of the few who take a longer range preventive view by doing what comes unnatural today so you can feel naturally better tomorrow. The following self-motivational statement reminders will prompt a longer range view of your love life, in the spirit of an ounce of prevention being worth a million pounds of cure.

- "No time like the present. If I give it my best shot in pleasing my mate, however awkward it might feel today, I will likely feel better tomorrow. After all, the more that I unnaturally do what pleases my mate, the more pleasant my mate and our relationship are likely to be."
- "Falling in love is like falling off a log; staying in love is like sawing a log. Nothing works but working. Better that I act against the grain of my natural inclinations so as to better accommodate my love life."
- "It's not easy to take the easy way out. Although it seems easier to regularly follow my natural inclinations, such a one-sided stance really hardens my ability to build bridges instead of walls with my partner."
- "Present pain for future gain. The effort required to incorporate measures that go against my grain but please my partner are best accepted as a small price to pay for mutual happiness gained."
- "As hard as it is to do, it's harder not to. Weaving rotation and balance into who gets their choice may seem a chore, but to not allow for such give-and-take will likely bring on even bigger difficulties."
- "Do I want to feel better now by insisting that I have my own way, or do I want to feel better for the duration of my relationship by promoting a more compatible balance in our relationship?"
- "Practice is the best teacher, and the more I practice going along with the grain of my mate's wishes, the more such activities are likely to seem naturally enjoying - in spite of myself!"
- "The first step is the hardest. The first time I do anything, including the first time I fight upstream against my natu-

ral personality tendencies in an effort to better bridge relationship gaps, will likely be the most difficult. Repeated efforts will likely result in more spontaneity."

- "Inspiration comes from perspiration, and if I'm waiting for something to turn up by way of relationship improvement, I had better start with my sleeves."

- "The line of least resistance is often the line of most resistance. Often, the hardest thing to give in a relationship is to give in. To offer less than such a workable compromise only makes me easier to resist in the long run."

- "Short-run sacrifices for long-run gains. The short-run sacrifice of bending without breaking by supporting rather than protesting against my mate's values paves the way for long-run gains of fuller relationship happiness and joy."

- "Don't wait for the tomorrows that never come. Start by getting started so as not to risk not getting started in getting a more favorable mood and move on in your relationship."

Maintaining and sustaining love while bridging compatibility gaps is not naturally easy. It can be made *easier* in the long run by doing today that which will produce more harmony tomorrow. Extending yourself beyond your natural boundaries, getting behind yourself and pushing, and fueling yourself with a philosophy of sustained effort may at first seem unnaturally unlike you. However, you may begin to like such a countermovement as it allows you to reap and encounter the natural loving fruits of your unnatural planting labor.

Note. From *Head Over Heart in Love: 25 Guides to Rational Passion* by Bill Borcherdt. Copyright © 1996, Professional Resource Exchange, Inc., P.O. Box 15560, Sarasota, FL 34277-1560.

Burying the Hatchet:
Open, Unadulterated
Apology as a Means
To Corrective Ends

Reaching out to apologize to a loved one is perhaps the shortest distance to thawing out icy feelings between two people. However, this mechanism of heating up the relationship had best be used as a springboard toward correcting wrongdoing rather than as an excuse to continue to use poor judgment. It's easier in the short run to confess to and apologize for errors that you have made than to admit to those that you fully intend to keep making. In other words, don't apologize as a means of temporarily pacifying your mate but as a strong commitment to doing better in the future. Focus on your corrective actions to come rather than the immediate comfort of open apology. Don't let the apology become an end in itself, but as a means of improvement in the future.

It is difficult to keep yourself angry at someone who openly apologizes for their misdeed and then makes an effort to correct it. It is also more fun to be around someone who is comfortable enough with himself or herself to lead with this method. Yet, in spite of its distinct advantages, direct, unqualified apology is a grossly underused method of getting on with the business of loving. To get yourself past the blocks to this underused portion of maintaining love requires a combination of identifying and understanding such obstacles and assertive action. What follows are barriers to breaking the apologetic ice and rational ideas that will assist you in getting out of the confessional *and* corrective starting blocks.

1. *Ego pride.* Thinking that if you define your conduct to be bad, you are also admitting that you are bad, will scare off any attempts to approach another with the humility that apologizing requires.

2. *Thinking being right as sacred and being wrong as bigger than life.* Until being right is taken off its pedestal and being wrong is seen as not being the worst of all possible crimes, apologizing will be cramped for space.

3. *Shame.* Fear of being subjected to social disapproval will startle and stifle efforts to lead with apologetic efforts to build bridges instead of walls.

4. *Fear of losing sexual gender.* Men are especially notorious for being little boys in big men's trousers by wrongly believing that their apologizing subtracts from their "masculinity."

5. *Thinking that apologizing is a sign of weakness.* Contrary to conventional wisdom, confessing to errors and apologizing for them is a sign of strength, not weakness; personal security, not insecurity.

6. *Fear of losing others' trust.* Assuming that if you openly apologize for your mistake, others will not trust you in the future, encourages you to not level in the present.

7. *Fear of being taken advantage of.* Anxiously assuming that when you apologize you open yourself up to more criticism from your social group in the future will cause you to hightail it away from such revealing possibilities.

8. *Fear of loss of respect.* Convincing yourself that apologizing for your admitted blunders will result in others' disrespect for you will also lead to your tending to avoid apologizing. Such hesitations unfortunately only serve to strengthen the original fear.

9. *Fear of discomfort.* Fearful overreaction to the emotional awkwardness that often accompanies doing something

that you have never or seldom done, including apologizing for a blunder, can discourage such an expressional effort.

10. *Specific irrational self-sentences that derail rational, apologetic action are:*

- "I shouldn't have to apologize, he should know that I'm sorry."
- "I'm not going to lower myself by apologizing."
- "I apologized last time around, this time it's her turn to."
- "If I apologize, he might think that he is better than me."
- "Love is never having to say you're sorry."
- "Nobody is ever going to get me to admit that I'm sorry."
- "If I admit to error and broadcast it by apologizing, no one will ever trust me again."
- "Saying I'm sorry and meaning it is too much out of character for me."
- "I'd feel so strange apologizing and I just couldn't stand such discomfort."
- "Apologizing for one wrongdoing will only open me up to be criticized for other things."
- "I'm a man, not a wimpy mouse - I'll be damned if I'm going to apologize!"
- "If I apologize to my mate, she will get the wrong idea and assume that I'm coming crawling back."

Each of these ideas reflects personal insecurities that can be overcome by vigorously expressing the following rational self-stated notions:

- "So if I feel nervous when apologizing, why would that be so ungodly hard to tolerate?"
- "Others will respect me for the same apologetic behavior that others will disrespect. You can't please them all."

- "Others might even trust me more if I'm honest and open enough to admit a mistake and unashamedly apologize for it."
- "How do I expect to ever correct my error if I don't at least admit it and offer some regret for making it?"
- "How can others know the regret I feel about my error unless I tell them? It seems like it's asking a lot for me to expect them to read my bloody mind."
- "Because I'm not used to apologizing doesn't mean that I can't get myself used to it."
- "Sincere apology is a sign of personality strength, not weakness."
- "Whatever wrong ideas others might give themselves about my apologies are not very important as long as I know what my right ideas are for doing so."
- "I am a man so I don't have to prove myself to be one by stubbornly refusing to land on the soft, apologetic side of my mistake."
- "Who cares whose turn it is, as long as the apologetic job gets done - so that then we may have more joy in our love life."
- "Love is a lot of things, including choosing to say you're truly sorry."
- "Better that I apologize; not to gloss over my mistakes but as a beginning commitment to correct them in the future."

The best can be yet to come! Thaw out your relationship with the melting effects of open apology. Use expressions of regret to make a clean sweep of your mistake and a fresh start in a new, more desirable direction. Stay away from qualifying expressions of sorrow such as:

- "Somebody has to apologize, so I suppose I may as well."
- "I'm sorry, even though I wasn't wrong."
- "I've always apologized in the past so I may as well do it now too."

- "Apology runs in my blood even though it doesn't yours, so here goes."
- "I'll do my duty and apologize."

Instead opt for straight, unadulterated fresh expressions of regret, such as:

- "I'm sorry. I plan to do better next time."
- "Will you forgive me for acting so foolishly?"
- "I really pulled a boner; I'm going to work hard at seeing that happens much less often."
- "That was a real error in judgment on my part. Please forgive me."
- "I didn't intend it to work out this way and I'm sorry that it did. Do forgive me."

The first several statements have hostile overtones - saying one thing and meaning another. Apologizing with animosity has the net effect of figuratively burying the hatchet - in the other's head and in the heart of the relationship. Make your apologies more than a token or resentful expression. This will more assure that the life of and in your relationship will last rather than die with a hatchet buried in its head and heart.

Note. From *Head Over Heart in Love: 25 Guides to Rational Passion* by Bill Borcherdt. Copyright © 1996, Professional Resource Exchange, Inc., P.O. Box 15560, Sarasota, FL 34277-1560.

What Would Possess Him
Or Her to Leave?
Possessiveness and Its
Paradoxical Effects

"To have and to hold" is a part of many marital vows. Yet, to do so in a possessive manner (e.g., "I have to have and hold you at all times that I desire") will destroy love's best intentions. Use of logic and reason to keep one's desires within reason is best done so as to not poison what one hopes to bring within one's clasp. Like the person who has grasped a butterfly in his or her hand, if the hand is tightened the butterfly will be injured, if not die. However, as soon as the grip is loosened the butterfly begins to thrive. The more of a grip you try to have on someone else's time and pleasure, the more you discourage that person from moving toward you. To try to tighten the reins on someone else's life as a method of attending to your own pleasures and insecurities is an immature, self-defeating method of forcing togetherness. The harder you try to force the possessive issue, the harder you make it for your love life to bloom.

Possessiveness refers to the childlike demand that others take it upon themselves to structure their time with and for you. The controller's philosophy is, "You are responsible for spending the best days of your life with me so that I can have the best days of my life in your presence, as this is the only manner in which I can do so." The fears that lie behind such a dependent philosophy and how not to get yourself caught up in another's emotional entanglements will now be reviewed. The statement "I wouldn't know what to do with my time without you, so show poor, little bitty old me the ways in which to spend my time" reflects the following fears and personality deficiencies:

1. *Fear of discomfort.* Facing the world with one's own re-sources can be associated with an exaggerated sense of discomfort. Therefore, to pacify my overconcern about feeling so uncomfortable, you must accompany me at practically any or all times.

2. *Fear of abandonment.* Infantile concerns that if you leave me to do something else, you might not come back are made to dominate. The fear here is not so much of losing another to a third party as losing out to other projects and activities that your partner might find more interest-ing than you.

3. *Fear of lacking creativity in a complex world.* Strongly sus-pecting that you don't have the creative wherewithal to find your own purposes in life can lead to a clinging ap-proach to the relationship.

4. *Fear of the unknown.* Not knowing what lies ahead and demanding that another do your forging ahead for you is an effort to get another to fight your battles for you because you have more than a sneaking suspicion that you are incapable of fighting your own.

5. *Mistrust of self.* "I trust you as far as I can throw you" is really a cover-up for "I don't trust myself as far as I can throw you to be able to enjoyingly structure the time of my life."

6. *Fear of infidelity.* Although most possessiveness reflects the discomfort associated with being alone, without di-rection from another, a portion of possessive insecurity is tied in with catastrophizing about the possibility of the other taking up with a different partner.

7. *Fear of failure.* "You are so much wiser and more success-ful than I, therefore I need to depend on you to make the

right decisions that I could never, as the failure that I am, make."

8. *Emotional dependency.* Possessiveness is rooted in neediness; that is, "I, dependent emotional cripple that I am, need you to sponsor me and my time." Such dependent yearnings create feelings of desperation that defeat love's interdependent, more free-wheeling ambitions.

9. *Feelings of inferiority.* Deficient self-evaluations leave one with no hope for less dependent self-improvements. After all, if I am so inferior to begin with, do I not have any other option but to continue to look to you in order to make something out of the time in my life?

10. *Fear of thinking more rationally.* Irrational thinking can be a rationalization for inaction. Such motives are motivated by the goal of immediate comfort. If the possessor starts to think more in terms of independent strivings, he or she may get his or her own attention, which means he or she may eventually end up rolling up his or her sleeves and going to work! Such a possibility is often viewed as too much of a loss of comfort and risk of failure. A quick decision is made to continue to be forever yielding to and dependent upon another. Bowing out from the effort required to be more dependent on self and less possessive of another is seen as a worthwhile exchange for the immediate convenience and comfort that comes from avoidance of necessary effort. Statements typically heard from insecure, possessive-acting people are:

- "Where are you going now?"
- "What do you expect me to do when you're gone?"
- "It seems like you would rather be away from than with me."
- "Seeing as you're gone so much, why don't you just carry a suitcase with you?"
- "How do you think I feel when you're gone - don't you even care?"

- "You are never around when I want to do something with you."
- "Can't I even go with you?"
- "Sure, go again - and let me sit."
- "Don't you ever feel guilty for leaving me alone?"
- "If you cared more about me you would spend more time with me."
- "Sometimes I think that you love your time away from me more than you love me."

It would be important not to let yourself be unduly influenced by such controlling stammerings. If you do, and end up increasingly sacrificing times of your life in the personal service of those whom you love, you will likely end up despising those whom you have sacrificed your time for. Better that you counter another's desperate, dependent yearnings by more rational self-talk, such as:

- "If I don't vie for time away from my partner, our love will be more likely to eventually die."
- "When I let my partner control me, we both lose control of what we originally hoped to bargain for in coming together."
- "One of the richest contributions I can make to our relationship is to not let either myself or my mate be the sole determiner of how we spend our time."
- "Sure my mate feels uncertain when we are apart - but who doesn't have problems? I can best help him with his problem by holding my ground and not giving in to such possessive activity."
- "Time away from each other will benefit both of us, even though I may be the only one who sees this right now."
- "How will my mate learn how to swim if I don't expect her to go into the water?"
- "If I give my mate a fish (by always being at arm's length), he will eat for today, but if I teach my mate how to fish (by forcing solitude upon him due to my absence), he will be more likely to be able to eat for a lifetime.

• "If I expect of my mate more than she expects of herself, I will be more likely to contribute to our relationship what we originally expected of it."

What would possess your mate to leave? Your possessive efforts to perfume your insecurity, that's what! Instead of falling into the possessiveness trap, strive to contribute to your, your mate's, and your relationship's growth and development by encouraging all concerned to grow up. Just as much can be learned from solitude, much can be learned and profited by time away from each other. Arrange for such absentee planning - whether or not your partner is presently mature enough to accept it. See that those fanatically possessed with a possessive solution to their insecurity want you to rescue them from their personal uncertainties. By possessing the stamina not to abide by their possessive callings, your relationship will more likely grow into producing the personal and interpersonal possessions that will aid it in better enduring the test of time.

Note. From *Head Over Heart in Love: 25 Guides to Rational Passion* by Bill Borcherdt. Copyright © 1996, Professional Resource Exchange, Inc., P.O. Box 15560, Sarasota, FL 34277-1560.

Looking for Fault But Not Blame With Infidelity

Fault means you are in violation; blame means condemning yourself for the violation. As applied to infidelity in love relationships, fault means that you have each likely contributed to incidents of unfaithfulness; blame reflects your condemnation of yourself, the other, or both for not supplying the conditions necessary to maintain fidelity. This chapter will try to encourage a nonblaming structure of understanding in the present and correction for the future so as to project hopes for what still can be for couples, both personally and interpersonally. In the aftermath of unfaithfulness, couples are usually too busy blaming themselves or projecting blame onto the other to identify their own faulty part in the plot; hence nothing is learned, because the fault goes unattended.

Although one partner may be a stronger contributor to fidelity violations, each would do well to find their faults without blaming themselves. Humans have a strong tendency to personalize. Mates who had their faithfulness values violated especially tend to make themselves feel hurtful, and by their view blameworthy. "What's wrong with me that my loved one turned to someone else? What a low-life person I am for letting myself be fooled into thinking that I was the highest on my mate's list of priorities." The violator of fidelity agreements is also likely to rate and condemn himself or herself as a low-life snake in the grass who deserves every licking that others' disapproval can bear. "What a schmuck of a subhuman entity am I for violating the fidelity arrange-

ment that we both agreed would be at the base of our relationship" is a statement that signals heavy doses of self-
condemnation. It would be better for both the transgressor
and the transgressed to examine the downfall of their vows
in a nonpersonalized, nonblaming manner. To pinpoint their
own faults without pinning blame would be the ideal to shoot
for. Each had best ask themselves, "What was it about our
relationship and my conduct in it that contributed to (him,
her, or me) taking up with someone else?" To use the incident as a learning experience by examining contributions from
both sides of the fence can be done by considering the following factors that contribute to infidelity:

1. *Quest for novelty.* Your mate may have lost the battle that
   humans have been fighting since day one - the security
   of monogamy versus the novelty of nonmonogamy. His
   or her loss of this battle may well have little or nothing to
   do with you or your conduct.
2. *Self-proving.* One way to make up for personal insecurities is to seek to prove yourself to be successful in other
   relationship contacts.
3. *One partner's inattention to the other's wants and to general
   relationship upkeep may make it convenient to look elsewhere
   for such desires.*
4. *Low frustration tolerance.* Convincing himself or herself
   that he or she is unable to tolerate the natural tedium
   that goes along with relationship routine can propel one
   mate to search for other options.
5. *General immaturity.* Not being able to grasp the value of
   long-term commitment to goals and projects can spill over
   into bypassing relationship agreements.
6. *Fickleness.* Whimsical attitudes that result in doing a little
   bit of a lot of things but not finding firm ground in any
   one of them can lead to a here-today, gone-tomorrow approach to love.
7. *Philosophies of problem avoidance.* Burying one's head in
   the sand at the onset of relationship problems allows them

to fester and multiply, sometimes in the direction of infidelity.

Underlying all these factors, whether you violated faithfulness or were violated against, is the importance of not defining yourself by your conduct or experience. That way you will be in a better position to stay on track with your life's goals while having the benefit of learning from rather than consuming your life by your mistakes. Rational ideas that will assist you in accomplishing that include:

- "My partner did what he did but is not what he did."
- "I did what I did, but I am not what I did."
- "My partner's conduct represents something my partner did; it does not represent me."
- "My conduct represents something that I did, it does not represent me."
- "My partner has some growing up to do, but I refuse to judge myself by her immaturity."
- "Now is a good time to attend to those problems that led to us drifting apart."
- "My mate acted in unfaithful ways in a manner that had to do with his natural tendencies rather than as a calculated effort against me."
- "I am sure I contributed to the present state of our relationship but I don't have to define myself, either by my negative contributions or by my mate's bad decisions to abandon our fidelity agreements."
- "Better that I use this incident as a means of examining and perhaps overhauling some of the ways I approach life and love."

As Dr. Albert Ellis, founder of rational emotive behavior therapy, points out in his book *The Civilized Couple's Guide to Extra-Marital Affairs* (1972), affairs are not necessarily bad for a relationship. They can be engaged in for right and wrong reasons, and they can offer distinct advantages for some couples some of the time. Infidelity by itself does not cause hurt or ruin relationships, although most unfaithfulness is followed by emotional hurt and relationship endings. Emotional disturbance about infidelity doesn't mean that the emotional disturbance was caused by the infidelity. The consequences of betrayal are determined more by whether individuals play their cards right. When fault is not sorted out from blame, what is likely to turn up is hurt, anger, and revenge. Separating these two often-related accusations allows you to turn down a lot of head- and heartache. Consequently, you will more clearheadedly be able to get a better bead on what went wrong, why, and what you can do about it, for the betterment of your relationship.

Note. From *Head Over Heart in Love: 25 Guides to Rational Passion* by Bill Borcherdt. Copyright © 1996, Professional Resource Exchange, Inc., P.O. Box 15560, Sarasota, FL 34277-1560.

Reasonable, Yet Unrealistic Love Expectations: Avoiding Their Toll and Toil

Knowing what to realistically expect of another human being is no small task. What you expect in your love relationship might be reasonable and therefore within the boundaries of fair play. Yet, your loved one may not have what it takes to play the game even within your permissive rules. Whether your expectations are met depends on another's capability to deliver. That's the rub. The trick is to exercise a decent respect for human limitations so as not to ask that your partner grasp beyond his or her reach. Happiness in and out of love is a direct ratio between what you expect and what you get. To improve your chances of being reasonable without being unrealistic, expect less. This chapter will contrast reasonable from unrealistic expectations in the service of more endearing and enduring companionship. It will also provide a listing of what to look for in a reasonable, realistic way in a love partner.

To pretend that love conquers all and therefore knows no boundaries is to invite problems and upsets. For instance, to expect you or your loving companion to be consistently affectionate, frugal, friendly, sensual, talkative, understanding, and interested in the other's projects may be barking up the wrong tree. Note that all of the preceding traits and characteristics are what is ordinarily considered reasonable, if not standard operating procedure for conventional social intercourse. However simple such requests are, they are not easy to provide. How and why is this so? Back to human short-comings and the value of accepting rather than protesting against them. To protest against the realities of ever-present human neglect of the reasonable is to be unrealistic in what to look for in another. Such disclaimers of reality produce abundant toll and toil, putting a heavy strain on love's resources and potential. If you demand that others know no boundaries to what they bring to the relationship, you are likely to anger yourself at them when they display their limits. By the same token, if you insist that you possess unlimited contributions to the relationship, you will put yourself down when you inevitably and frequently fall short of the perfectionistic bull's-eye. Such refusals to accept the grim realities of contrasting what is reasonable of people generally, yet unrealistic for *this* person, are seen in the following intolerant and nonaccepting ideas:

- "Because I ask for so little, my requests *must* be honored."
- "I know he could be different if he really wanted to, and therefore he should change."
- "I provide and change for her, therefore she *must* provide for and change for me."
- "Reasonable requests *should* get reasonable results."
- "People should get what they give. I give, so therefore I *should* get."
- "How can he be so unreasonable about my simple requests? I *must* know why!"
- "My requests are so simple and easy that I *shouldn't* even have to ask."
- "She knows how important these requests are for me and therefore *must* comply."
- "I'm only asking for a few crumbs and *should* be able to gain such a little taster."
- "When I expect the moon, negligence is excusable, but when I opt for a favor that's within reason, I *must* gain it."
- "He *must not* betray my reasonable requests!"

- "She knows I hurt when deprived of simple pleasures from her and therefore she *must not* do so."
- "If my partner truly loved and respected me he *would* find a way to provide me with such small favors."

Contrasting ideas that serve to avoid the emotional anguish that follows from demanding expectations that may be generally reasonable, though unrealistic for this individual, are:

- "Where is it written that simply because I ask for so little I must gain what I seek?"
- "Even if he could provide more, it doesn't mean that he should or has to!"
- "There is no evidence that because I provide for others' requests, they must give me a return on my investment!"
- "How can she be so unreasonable about my simple requests?" "EASILY, that's how!"
- "Others' negligence of my wants is to be expected; after all, I don't run the universe yet!"
- "Whether my partner favorably or unfavorably considers my requests may well have nothing to do with his love for me."
- "So I don't get what I think that I reasonably deserve; it's unrealistic to demand that I must!"
- "Expect less, get more!"
- "Give yourself fewer expectations of others and you will have fewer complaints about others!"
- "Don't expect to not be short-changed if you expect your relationship to last a long time!"

If one is to be reasonable yet realistic in expectations of others, what is one to rightly look for in a potential mate? Keep in mind that it would be important to bargain, though in perhaps less of a degree than one would like, for one's deepest wishes, wants, and desires - but not for too hard of a bargain in asking what *this* partner under consideration might not be capable of providing.

The following are traits and features to look for within the capability of a potential love/marital partner:

1. *Someone who is emotionally disturbed, admits it, and is willing to work against inborn tendencies such as overreacting and taking things personally. All* humans possess emotional disturbance. A few will admit to it and fewer will work hard to control such natural-born distractions.

2. *High frustration tolerance (HFT).* Staying in love and marriage is the supreme test of patience. This is why couples who elope out of impatience are likely beat before they start on the long-term journey to follow.

3. *Someone who knows what they want to do when they grow up.* Mating with a person who has found a sense of fulfillment in his or her work makes for a more fulfilling match.

4. *A sense of humor.* A couple who laughs together, stays together - provided they laugh with each and not at each other.

5. *Sees their parents for what they are, in their flaws and shortcomings.* Such realism lessens possibilities of over-attachments to them.

6. *Is encouraging of your personal development and pleasures.* Seek a mate who is interested not only in what you can do for him or her, but actively pursues an interest in what you can do for yourself.

7. *A person you can depend on without being dependent upon and vice versa.* The reliability factor builds appreciation while dependency breeds resentment.

8. *Agreement on children.* Decisions regarding whether to have them, how many, and methods of management in the event of their presence can save a lot of emotional wear, tear, and tears.

9. *Common religious or nonreligious base.* Options of religious affiliation/denomination/personal beliefs about this matter or, on the other hand, to abstain from such ideology is an important factor in how much of a rocky road lies ahead.

10. *Valuing of interdependence.* Finding someone who wants to connect with you but not fuse with you is another factor in establishing smoother going. Balancing the you, me, and us of your relationship is a juggling act that tries to stay away from bending over backwards to please and placate another, demanding that the other make a strenuous effort to continually please you. Instead, it seeks give and take, rotation and balance, where you try to please yourself and the other some of the time.

11. *Takes a noncommercialized view of love.* Living with someone who treats love as if it were a soap opera, making himself or herself desperately dependent on getting it and hurt, angry, and betrayed when he or she doesn't get it is like walking on thin ice. Choosing someone who is not demanding, commanding of, and desperate for love provides more of a solid footing in your life's and love's journey.

12. *A sense of optimism.* It is more fun to be around someone who regularly seeks out the good in life, even in those things that are by appearance bad.

13. *Someone who is of a natural interlocking temperament and value system with you.* Preferably look for a mate who, without trying too hard, naturally coordinates with your personality and fairly easily agrees with you regarding what constitutes the good life. As noted in a previous chapter, opposites attract - and attack. People change their preferences little over time. What you see is what you get. Try to find someone who likes to play the same games in the same ballparks as you.

14. *Personality well-roundedness.* Someone who has many enjoying pursuits is likely to be less dependent on the relationship, consequently straining it less.

15. *Someone who is **not** in love with himself or herself.* People who love themselves can oftentimes be very syrupy. Beyond that distracting mushy annoyance they are often incapable of understanding others because they are too busy overfocusing on and trying to prove themselves.

16. *Approaches life with a sense of mastery.* Associating with someone who tries to figure out the mechanics of his or her personal/interpersonal/intimate life can prove interesting. People constantly searching for answers are stimulating to be around.

17. *Can give and take no for an answer.* Long-range resentments can be nipped in the bud when someone is bold enough to give and secure enough to take no for an answer.

18. *Appreciates variety, as such is the spice of life.* Someone who likes to try new things, walk different paths, play with different ideas can be a welcome addition in and to your life.

19. *Finds self-change challenging.* People who are ready and willing to look at parts of their personality that they would like to smooth off and then nondefensively find excitement in fine-tuning those portions can be encouraging for the purpose of your own search of self.

20. *Moderate spending habits.* Looking for those who don't spend money that they don't have, yet are willing to spend some of the money they have is a delicate balance that prevents going through life by the seat of one's financial pants.

21. *Someone who delights in getting more bees with honey than with vinegar.* Moving toward someone who is naturally interested in being emotionally nourishing, supportive, and compassionate is a real treat.

22. *Determinedly avoids self- and other definitions.* Those who make it a point to not give themselves a report card with a good mark for doing the right things and a bad mark for doing the wrong things avoids depression and self-hate. Not using the same rating system with others prevents anger and other-hate. Steering clear of these negative emotions saves a lot of headaches and heart troubles.

23. *Disagrees in a civilized manner.* People differ, and differences tend to clash, but the intensity of the sound can be

kept down to a roar when individuals tell how they think and feel without telling you off.

24. *Strives for undamning acceptance.* Someone who can accept the inconveniences, uncertainties, annoyances, and hassles of other people and of life generally without damning them provides opportunities for them to influence people and circumstances to change, when possible. With undamning acceptance of self, others, and life practically always comes hope.

Examine the preceding compatibility factors, and decide if you want to bargain for some, many, or most, keeping in the back of your head a decent respect for accepting this person's limitations in meeting them. Some of these resources would be conditions of the relationship without which there would be no relationship. Determine which ones would be acceptable to you and to what degree. Explain to your partner what you have concluded so that he or she can decide his or her readiness, willingness, and ability to meet them. Suggest that he or she provide you with the same compatibility analysis regarding what the conditions of the relationship future are for him or her. Then, if you can honestly say to yourselves that you have itemized and prioritized in a reasonable, realistic manner, test your conclusion as to what you both believe to be the raw materials necessary to more fully build your relationship; discovering for yourself if reasonableness and realism can be brought together as the toll to pay, while avoiding the toil of your personal and interpersonal well-being.

Note. From *Head Over Heart in Love: 25 Guides to Rational Passion* by Bill Borcherdt. Copyright © 1996, Professional Resource Exchange, Inc., P.O. Box 15560, Sarasota, FL 34277-1560.

APPENDIX

I've Got the Fever, But Do You Really Have the Cure? Love Dependency: Complexities, Complications, And Corrections*

People have some funny ideas about love that are quite sad. Many of these faulty notions are based on:

1. *The short-range convenience of staying in a love relationship even when it is more harmful than not.* Much of what is called "love addiction" is really a self-created dependency on immediate comfort. When the adjustment process of leaving an unsatisfying relationship is viewed as being more difficult than staying in it, the status quo becomes the pathway of choice. Those who opt for this line of least resistance will do so until the immediate pain of everyday incompatibility outweighs the fear of the long-range unknown. Matters are allowed to get worse before they get better before realizing that frustration doesn't have to mount before taking forward-looking action. Fear of immediate discomfort and shortsightedness result in

*Note. From *You Can Control Your Feelings! 24 Guides to Emotional Well-Being* (pp. 195-213) by Bill Borcherdt. Copyright © 1993, Professional Resource Exchange, Inc., P.O. Box 15560, Sarasota, FL 34277-1560.

attachment to the rush of instant relief that is experienced from putting off until tomorrow what has already been put off until today. Love junkies are really comfort junkies in disguise. Exaggerating the pain that is required to leave a dead-end relationship while basking in the short-run security of maintaining the familiar does not allow a dead relationship to get a decent burial.

2. *Self-judgments in proportion to the quality of one's love life.* Measuring oneself as favorable when among the very loving and as unfavorable when on the outside looking in to love possibilities leads to emotional entrapment. Without a love baseline you are likely to depress yourself about lacking the necessary prop to increase your self-estimation. With love in hand, anxiety about being without your sacred measure that would lead to self-diminishment is likely to dominate.

3. *Unquestioning reliance on commercialized platitudes.* These sound comforting but come up short in the midst of everyday elbow-rubbing realities. It is as if believers of the Hollywood drama don't want to be told the truth about love, even though the truth would mean the freedom to think and to choose in a more flexible, well-thought-out manner what foundation they would like to lay for intimate relationships.

4. *Mistaken ideas about what love or lack of it can or cannot do to and for a person.* All-or-nothing beliefs that love can either build you up or tear you down put you at the mercy of one dimension of your life and block a more well-rounded view of self.

People raise their emotional temperatures for these described reasons: temporary convenience, self-evaluation, gullibility to media's unrealistic portrayals, and absolute expectations regarding love's advantages. Consequently they expose themselves to such emotional hazards as fear, anger, guilt, and depression. Matters are then made more complicated by the practical disadvantages of driving others away.

Desperate, upset people are not much fun to be around, and often they find that they do not blend well with those whom they wish to become closer to. Although they longingly look to others to supply the cure for the dependency that ails them, their other-directed methods defeat the purpose of their good intentions. They rightly form attachments and then wrongly rely on exclusive return attachments to support their original investment. Finding little value in themselves, they look to others to supply their emotional fix.

To moderate love's passion made dependent, let's examine the ways of thinking that trigger such rising heartfelt temperatures. Such an overview has the advantage of building one's love relationships on the rock of self-sufficiency rather than on the sand of dependence on others. Following is a list of 26 irrational ideas about love. "Irrational" is defined as notions that cannot be verified with evidence. Each irrational belief (IB) is followed by (a) a faulty self-statement (FSS) that tries to document the thought but leads to interfering emotions (IE); (b) countering self-statements (CSS) that argue against the original unprovable idea so as to lead to more favorable feelings (FF); and (c) general comment (GC) about the rational background philosophy of each manner of thinking, feeling, and acting.

1. IB: *Love is a dire need that unless met will create utter and profound misery.*

   FSS: "I need love and therefore would be devastated without it."
   IE: Fear, anxiety.
   CSS: (a) "Love may be one of the nicest things that I could experience, but nice doesn't mean necessary"; (b) "True, I would feel sad without love in my life but I wouldn't have to turn that disappointment into a disaster"; (c) "There is evidence that I very much want love but there is no universal truth that says it is a requirement for my life."

FF: Healthy concern and anticipation.

GC: Striving for what you value in life is the substance out of which much meaning is created. Thinking that you have to have (need) what you find highly desirable takes you from being vitally involved in pursuing love's advantages to becoming emotionally entangled in gaining what you prize. Consequently, you will likely clumsily defeat your own purposes while driving others away with your desperation.

2. IB: *Love is a valid indicator of personal worth.*

FSS: "Love increases my self-worth and makes me a better and good person (while being without it decreases my self-worth and makes me a worse and a bad person)."

IE: Depression, guilt.

CSS: (a) "In some ways love results in my being better off, but having love's advantages does not turn me into a better person"; (b) "My love life does not represent me. It is one of the many projects that I will participate in during my lifetime. I'd best not judge myself by any one of them or I will put my emotions at the mercy of my successes or failures"; (c) "Self-evaluation is immoral in that it leads to hurting myself: If I estimate myself to have more worth when my love life is going strong, I will judge myself to be bad when my love life could or begins to falter."

FF: Emotional relief, peacefulness, clearheadedness.

GC: Love-life problems are often problems of self-evaluation. Giving yourself a report card with a high mark when able to gain favorable love experiences leads to giving yourself that same report card with a low mark when experiencing less-than-hoped-for love advantages. Emotional flip-flopping can be set aside by strongly understanding that you are not your love life and that having love doesn't make you superhuman any more than not having it makes you subhuman. Self-judgments will throw cold water on even the best of love relationships. You will likely worry about losing what you have made the sacred estimate of your life, fearfully blundering on in attempting to retain this essential factor.

3. IB: *Love is both natural and naturally easy.*

   FSS: "Because love is such a natural thing I shouldn't have to work very hard to maintain it - if I fall into love I should fall into happiness."
   IE: Complacency, listlessness, lethargy, inertia.
   CSS: (a) "I'd best see that although falling in love is like falling off a log, maintaining it is more like sawing a log: The only thing that works is working"; (b) "Although I can easily attach myself to a love partner, I had better work hard at maintaining that attachment"; (c) "Little comes easy but trouble, and that's exactly what I'm likely to give myself unless I accept that love's inspiration is often a companion of persistent perspiration."
   FF: Alertness, vigor, motivation.
   GC: People often have problems in their love relationships not so much because they change, but because they stubbornly refuse to change. Refusing to give up the impossible dream of eternal bliss served on a silver platter leads to a childish refusal to put oneself through the toil that is often required to keep a good thing going well.

4. IB: *Love and agreement, compatibility, and/or obligation are sacredly linked and therefore by necessity go together.*

   FSS: "Those who love me are required to always agree with, support, and console me and oblige my every request and desire. I in turn must make like provisions for them. If by chance either of us falters in these statutory commitments, it is to be viewed as a breach of loyalty and means one loves the other less."

IE: Guilt by the violator; betrayal and anger by the receiver.

CSS: (a) "In many ways it is better when my partner and I are in sync with our opinions and wishes. However, because we are not clones of one another it is natural that this will not always be the case"; (b) "Not believing ourselves to be servants of one another's wishes will make for a relationship based on choice rather than compulsion. Such loosening up of duty-bound beliefs will afford us less dependency and more carefreeness"; (c) "By agreeing to disagree we can learn much from one another in our different opinions."

FF: Tolerance, acceptance, grace, forgiveness.

GC: Love does not conquer all, and it is not the answer to everything - including incompatibility. People are different, and to think that these differences violate love ties invites emotional fallout. Uniting varying tastes can be like trying to fit round pegs into square holes. Although better accommodating individual differences is preferable it cannot always be done. Couples would do well to stay away from the notion "Agree with what I have to say or you don't love me." Relationships that do not stand the test of controversy probably won't stand the test of time.

5. IB: *Love must be reciprocal, and when it is not the other is to be condemned and punished as a rotten person.*

FSS: "If I take the time and energy to attach myself to someone else, especially if I go out of my way to

treat him with no lapses in kindness and consideration, he is required to give me a return on my
investment. If he does not return the favor, I'll hate
his guts until the day he dies - and I hope it's soon."

IE: Betrayal, anger, hurt, hostility.

CSS: (a) "Others have free will - not my will. My choice
is whether to bond with them. Their choice is
whether to return the bonding. They may make
what I view to be a bad choice, but that does not
make them bad"; (b) "People have a right to select
and discriminate against me as much as I have a
right to make myself biased toward them"; (c) "Attaching myself to someone else is not to be taken
lightly. However, because I put forth the effort to
connect emotionally with them does not mean they
are required to do the same."

FF: Keen but healthy disappointment, regret, sadness.

GC: Many people fall in love as a childish excuse to
insist on reciprocation. The invented reverse
golden rule of "others have to do unto me as I do
unto them" had best be uninvented. The fact that
someone is on a different wavelength as you does
not constitute a federal crime and does not qualify
him or her for the scum bucket.

6. *IB: Love has the power to destroy you.*

FSS: "I'm at the emotional mercy of the status of my
love life. When I extend my love efforts my life is
controlled/determined by that status. Because I
am at the mercy of my love experiences, they are
to be feared and approached with extreme caution."

IE: Anxiety, fear, stress, tension.

CSS: (a) "Although it is doubtful I would be unflappable
in the throes of love disappointments, I would not
have to do an emotional tilt in the event of such
disenchantment"; (b) "I'm not a trained seal, rat,

or guinea pig. Thus, I can think for myself in ways that can allow me not to turn sadness into tragedy"; (c) "Negative results in my love life can only dissatisfy and frustrate me; only by exaggerating the significance of these can I make myself disturbed."

FF: Healthy concern, apprehension, confidence.

GC: Events do not cause emotions. Beliefs about those events do. Emotions verify what you believe about a circumstance. Curtailing overreactive thoughts by viewing matters in deliberate and not desperate ways permits you to override, rather than be overridden by, love's happenings. Your emotions do not represent your love life but rather your beliefs about your love life.

7. IB: *Love means getting yourself upset about your loved one's problems and disturbances.*

FSS: "If my partner is upset I have to get myself at least equally upset. If I don't that means I love her less and that is a breach of my undying loyalty to the relationship. In addition, for not putting myself in a similar bad emotional way, I'm a bad partner and/or person."

IE: Guilt, depression.

CSS: (a) "My level of upset about my partner's concerns has nothing to do with the price of tamales as far as my love for her. In fact, not taking her as seriously as she is taking herself may be an act of love in itself"; (b) "Part of love is trying to be helpful in the time of your partner's adversity. The less upset I make myself, the more clearheadedly helpful I will likely be."

FF: Composure, deliberation.

GC: Upsetting oneself and then having two people upset about the same thing is not the loving, helpful thing to do. Getting rid of this narrow equation - more upset = more caring - helps moderate the amount of feeling that is against the relationship's best interest.

8. IB: *The only alternative to love is loneliness, and therefore lack of love has to lead to despair.*

> FSS: "Being without love means being without anything and everything. If I'm alone there is nothing I can do to prevent loneliness and distress from setting in. When love's gone - I'm a goner."
>
> IE: Depression, worry, anxiety.
>
> CSS: "Being without someone doesn't mean being without anything. In fact, if I play my cards right I can take advantage of the increased freedom and choices of going solo. My being alone will not lead to any place in particular other than where I direct it."
>
> FF: Anticipation, challenge, excitement.
>
> GC: Being alone is often turned into the self-fulfilling promise of loneliness. Much can be experienced and learned from solitude if favorable options are not blocked by deterministic thinking.

9. IB: *Overcoming fear of losing in love can be done by withdrawing from involvements.*

> FSS: "If I try to gain mutual love I'm afraid I might fail. For me to get over this fear it is best that I avoid all appearances of what I am afraid of because then it will go away by itself."
>
> IE: Worry, fear, anxiety, desperation.
>
> CSS: (a) "By consistently taking my fears with me and exposing myself to the possibility of losing the love I am afraid of losing, I will likely develop an immunity to my fears"; (b) "A good way to overcome

my fear of losing out in love is to convince myself of the truth - that such an occurrence would be bearable rather than terrible, horrible, and catastrophic"; (c) "I won't learn how to swim by knowing that I am required to get into the water and move my arms; it would be best if I actually did it. So too, I won't learn love-seeking skills by just thinking about them - I would do better to develop a philosophy of actual participation and nonavoidance."

FF: Anticipation, confidence, deliberation.

GC: Purposeful, fearful avoidance of an activity often makes it appear bigger than life. Making contact with the same happening (especially repeatedly) brings it clearer into focus as a part of life. The further you go into the mouth of the dragon, the less you are likely to fear the dragon.

10. IB: *Love is a 50-50 proposition.*

FSS: "My partner should do his half of the relationship work, and I should do mine. This will result in us living happily ever after. If by chance our tabulations don't turn out to be 'Even Stephen' it can only be interpreted as one maliciously taking advantage of the other."

IE: Betrayal, self-pity, resentment.

CSS: (a) "It is nice when my partner and I both work together on our relationship, but it is not necessary that we keep score of our efforts"; (b) "For us to be in never-ending sync we would have to be perfect. Perfectionism is not a human trait; it would be wise to expect and accept our faults"; (c) "Relationships are more like 60-40, 30-70, or 80-20 depending on the daily effort of each partner - it would be best for me to allow for this range of human variability and inequality."

FF: Appropriate annoyance and disappointment, forgiveness.

GC: A certain amount of reasonable inequality had best be accepted in any relationship. To try to perfectly fine-tune a relationship can only multiply existing frustrations.

11. IB: *Love is more trouble than it's worth.*

FSS: "Gaining and maintaining a love relationship is such a hassle, I'll take on an attitude of 'I don't care, what's the difference?' It's just too strenuous to get into the act of love so I'll just sit on the sidelines and pretend it doesn't matter."

IE: Casualness, listlessness, lethargy, inertia.

CSS: (a) "Like any project worth its salt, love requires lots of energy. Sometimes such effort will pay off, sometimes it won't. However, meaning can be gained by trying, which can take on a life of its own. Succeeding, which would be frosting on the cake, is always an additional worthwhile possibility"; (b) "Like most humans, I have a strong preference for closeness and affection. Finding such experiences at times may seem futile. However, why not go for more of the marbles and put my efforts into what I prize at a higher level rather than toward a lesser value? What better way to spend my time than to actively seek out what is important to me"; (c) "Taking a flippant, casual view toward what I value in life is not going to intensify my existence."

FF: Motivation, vital absorption, increased energy.

GC: Acting like something really doesn't matter when it really does often disguises a fear of failure and anguish about the pain that one will be required to put oneself through to accomplish a goal. Some comfort can be found in a laid-back mentality that camouflages failure and discomfort anxieties.

12. IB: *Past failure experiences in love must have a strong influence on how you continue to love, indefinitely.*

    FSS: "Because I have previously floundered in my love relationships I will continue to falter, because the past sets the groundwork for the present and future."

    IE: Resignation, depression, lethargy, hopelessness.

    CSS: (a) "I can learn from my past failures rather than repeat them"; (b) "The past is a bridge to the present, but it does not determine the present or future"; (c) "It is just as important to learn what doesn't work in building love relationships as it is to discover what does; my failures have taught me just that."

    FF: Hope, anticipation, courage, inspiration.

    GC: Failing has advantages when you play your cards right. Putting what you've learned from your flaws in the past to good use can help you to succeed in present relationships. To believe that the past is the master of your future makes for an uninspired viewpoint on love with a mind closed to more favorable outcomes.

13. IB: *Without love you have nothing at all.*

    FSS: "Love is everything; without it I could not find any value to myself or discover any enjoyment in life."

    IE: Fear, worry, anxiety, panic, depression.

    CSS: (a) "Love is one of the better if not near the best things I could have going for myself. However, as big a part of my life as it might be, it is not bigger than my life"; (b) "If one part of my life (such as love) wavers, it does not mean that the rest is required to extinguish"; (c) "With love I have one set of advantages; without love I have a different range of advantages. It would be best for me to focus on those dimensions that I have going for me at the present moment in my life."

FF: Appreciation, happiness, joy.

GC: Commercialized views of love would like you to believe that love is the alpha and omega to a satisfying existence. Using all-or-nothing thinking to make sacred the value love has for you will likely be emotionally disruptive for your love-seeking purposes.

14. IB: *Human beings have an unlimited capacity to give and receive love.*

FSS: "I should be able to provide, and others should be able to supply me, an unlimited supply of love. If either of us falters in achieving our fullest potential we are to be condemned for not placing among the very loving."

IE: Guilt, anxiety, depression.

CSS: (a) "I'd best give myself the benefit of the doubt and have a decent respect for, though not an intimidation of, human limitations. I am limited in whatever I do - including my ability to give and receive provisions of love"; (b) "It is regretful when I find myself not being able to provide or receive the amount of love I would like. However, this deficiency does not constitute a calamity"; (c) "If I don't put so much pressure on myself I may well be able to lighten up while opening up my availability to send and receive love."

FF: Peacefulness, clearheadedness, acceptance.

GC: Love is not at the fingertips of all who wish to create and experience it. Love is a very desirable experience for most. As soon as we insist that we have to experience what is favorable we lose sight of our limited potential, put undue pressure on ourself to do what we can only allow - not force -

ourself to do, and block ourself from letting what
capacity we do have show through.

15. IB: *Love relationships should not have conditions attached to
         them.*

    FSS: "If I really love someone there will be no conditions
          attached to our relationship. If I do impose condi-
          tions this means (a) I love the other less, and (b)
          I'm being selfish. True love means giving until it
          hurts and then giving some more with no expecta-
          tion in return."
    IE: False hopes, ultimate betrayal and self pity, guilt.
    CSS: (a) "Because I wish some profit and advantage from
          my love relationships means I care enough about
          them to gain from them so I can then more conve-
          niently give to them"; (b) "By defining my wants I
          encourage give-and-take and discourage the atti-
          tude of taking for granted, resulting in a variety of
          experiences for both of us - and variety is one of
          the spices of love"; (c) "By getting my partner to
          respond to me instead of one-sidedly responding
          to her I am encouraging rotation and balance in
          the everyday interactions out of which mutually
          satisfying relationships are carved"; (d) "By increas-
          ing my leverage and bargaining power I will likely
          put myself in a better position to gain in my love
          life. I can then reinvest this profit for the benefit of
          both of us."
    FF: Security, confidence, realistic optimism.
    GC: Far from being selfish, expecting provisions from
          your partner is of benefit to your partner, you, and
          the relationship. It is fair to your partner because
          he or she now knows what is important for you
          and doesn't have to guess as to how to warm the
          cockles of your heart. Once he or she meets your
          expectations he or she will have the added benefit

of finding you more fun to be around. It is to your advantage to be the recipient of your partner's desirable conduct. The relationship itself is likely to pay dividends from your favorable social exchange agreements and follow-through.

16. IB: *Love conquers all.*

   FSS: "Love is like my guardian angel - everything will be all right because of it."
   IE: False hopes, complacency, lethargy.
   CSS: (a) "Love is important, but it will not move mountains nor perform major surgery on individual differences with my partner"; (b) "Love is not a magical potion. It is not to be viewed as a substitute for the hard work necessary to carve out compromises on matters of mutual concern"; (c) "Falling into love is not the same as falling into happiness. The latter is to be worked out, worked on, and worked at rather than be seen as happening automatically."
   FF: Incentive, realistic anticipation and participation.
   GC: Humans tend to direct themselves toward what appears easier. Commercialized views of love make it convenient to view eternal happiness as an automatic companion to love. Love sustained comes from the ingenuity and hard work necessary to make yourself hard to resist. Love as a never-ending conqueror overlooks this grim - but not too grim - reality.

17. IB: *If after much frustration you decide to stop loving someone, you're a failure.*

   FSS: "I've put so much into this relationship and I've gotten nearly nothing in return, but if I fail to complete what I started I'd be a failure and couldn't live with or by myself."

IE: Insecurity, fear, guilt.

CSS: (a) "Finally realizing that it's time to stop trying to revive a dead relationship is something to rejoice about rather than put myself down about"; (b) "I can do myself a favor by dropping the ball if the ball game has long been over"; (c) "Everybody makes mistakes but I don't have to continue to make mine."

FF: Surety, confidence, emotional relief.

GC: Taking a bad situation and not making it worse - not duplicating a mistake - stems from admitting your poor judgment to begin with combined with the resolve to start over. Seeing that your original failure does not represent you permits movement in a more promising direction.

18. IB: *Love increases sexual arousal.*

FSS: "Because love and sex are so natural they should come together naturally easy. Love equals sex; therefore, if one is good, the other should be, too. Romantic love makes for romantic sex - no way should I be required to inconvenience myself to enjoy sex - rather than do that I'll roll over and go to sleep."

IE: Resentment, high frustration, complacency, lethargy.

CSS: (a) "If I wish to heighten my sexual arousal I'd best do what would be compatible with that goal - focus on my physiology and special sexy thoughts - after the sex I can focus on how much I love my partner"; (b) In sex, or any other worthwhile endeavor, little works but working"; (c) "In many ways love is incompatible with and a distraction to sex; if I don't keep my mind on what is sexy for me, how can I expect to achieve sexual ends?"

FF: Motivation, incentive, anticipation, acceptance.

GC: Although it is more convenient to believe that love will naturally increase sexual arousal with little energy output it does not stand the test of a law of learning. If you are going to accomplish a goal you are likely to be required to vigorously focus on the substance of your objective rather than sidetrack yourself. If you are eating a gourmet meal and you focus on how much you love the cook rather than relishing each morsel of the food he or she has prepared you will likely enjoy the meal less. Likewise, if you focus on loving thoughts, your sexual appetite will likely diminish.

19. IB: *Love means always understanding (without explanation or request).*

FSS: "After all this time if my partner really loved me he would know what I want without me having to ask."

IE: Resentment, self-pity, anger.

CSS: (a) "If my partner were a mind reader he would have gotten rich on the stock market by now"; (b) "Where is it written that my partner has to draw me out, baby me, pamper me, or in any other manner, shape, or form read my bloody mind"; (c) "Am I helpless or so lazy that I can't let my wants be known without wrongly thinking that my partner is supposed to do my work for me?"

FF: Self-initiative, motivation.

GC: Mates have enough of their own desires to monitor without being expected to stay one step ahead of yours. This irrational belief is rooted in the childish insistence upon unending protection and being taken care of.

20. IB: *Love means always saying yes.*

FSS: "If you really love me you will always cater to my wishes and never say no."

IE: Resentment, anger, self-pity, hurt.

CSS: (a) "Others have free will, not my will"; (b) "Because I like to be accommodated by my partner does not mean that she is obliged to do so"; (c) "There is no evidence that what is important to my partner as it contrasts to what is important to me has anything to do with her love for me."

FF: Patience, tolerance, acceptance.

GC: The tendency to take someone's refusal of a request personally accounts for the hurt that follows such a turning away. This insistent irrational idea that love means that under all conditions you must not deny my request, attempts to perfume such potential discomfort.

21. IB: *If you love someone you don't use him.*

FSS: "If he really loved me he wouldn't expect advantages, conveniences, or favors from me."

IE: Resentment, bitterness, despisement.

CSS: (a) "Why is it so unusual for people to search for profit, gain, and advantage from those they love?"; (b) "Expecting profits from a love relationship keeps interest high, discourages taking the relationship for granted, and encourages give-and-take"; (c) "It is nice to give *and* receive; why must my partner not have a strong preference for both?"

FF: Understanding, caring, acceptance.

GC: The very reason we permit ourselves to fall in love is to use what provisions our partner affords. Love is a convenience item - it is convenient to fall in love with someone when they please us by the assets they provide for our use (e.g., looks, intelligence, creativity, humor, etc.). If partners didn't expect such provisions from one another there would be less motivation to make themselves harder to resist by putting their best foot forward.

22. IB: *My partner has to admit she is wrong and change before I can be happy.*

    FSS: "My mate makes me upset and therefore is responsible for my feelings. She must admit what she is doing to me so that I can then live happily ever after."

    IE: Anger, hostility, resentment.

    CSS: (a) "Nobody has ever invented a way to change somebody else - I'd best put my money down on: 'My, how you have changed since I have changed' "; (b) "Because one part of my life is not going well does not mean that the rest has to go down the tubes"; (c) "If I'm not accountable and responsible for my own problems, who is? Better that I not put my personal happiness at the mercy of someone else's conduct lest I live my life on an emotional shoestring."

    FF: Self-reliance, tolerance, self-confidence, clear-headedness.

    GC: Happiness is not externally caused. You don't have to make yourself dependent on circumstances and people to change before you can begin to experience more of the joys and less of the hassles of life.

23. IB: *Love means always telling others what they want to hear.*

    FSS: "I am responsible for my partner's feelings. Therefore, I should only say things that I know he is going to take kindly to. Besides, I can't stand it when he voices his upset."

    IE: High stress, fear, guilt, other-pity.

    CSS: (a) "If I can't make my partner happy I can't make him miserable either"; (b) "By assuming my mate would be an emotional cripple in the face of my honest opinion I am not giving him my confidence nor encouraging him to develop to his fuller emotional potential"; (c) "Not rocking the boat can sometimes lead to the kind of peace found in grave-yards. If our love cannot tolerate the test of dis-agreement, perhaps we'd best look at its weak links more closely."

FF: Goodwill, other-confidence, less stress and strain.

GC: Being honest - under the umbrella of saying what the other wants to hear - is not likely to be the sub-stance of which long-term relationships are made. Some degree of open, honest, level-headed discus-sions are helpful if couples more fully wish to get to know and trust one another.

24. IB: *Love means always being totally honest.*

FSS: "No matter what the potential consequences I must always be totally honest with my partner; if I should intentionally or unintentionally slip this would mean that I love her less."

IE: Anxiety, guilt.

CSS: (a) "I'd do well to distinguish between a white lie and a black truth. Just as I would not give my mate a food she was allergic to, I would think twice about saying something that she would predictably over-react to"; (b) "Show me a relationship where a cer-tain amount of catering doesn't go on, and I'll show you a relationship that's made in heaven - and I know of no relationships that are made in heaven"; (c) "Respecting another's unfortunate sore spots enough to tip-toe around them can be a loving thing to do."

FF: Respect, tolerance, forgiveness.

GC: There are exceptions to practically every rule. Be-cause a trait such as honesty is preferable does not mean that it has to be compulsively applied. Like anything else, use it only when it is to the long-range advantage of you and your love life.

25. IB: *When two people love each other there is invariably a right, precise, perfect solution to each of their problems and it is catastrophic when this is not found.*

   FSS: "Well-intended love will take care of problems, regardless of whether it is backed by the right methods. How humongously awful it would be if this did not turn out to be the case."

   IE: High frustration, guilt, heightened anguish.

   CSS: (a) "Why is it so strange, and why do I have to make myself feel so disheartened, when we can't unlock the secret to all our problems and concerns?"; (b) "Is it really sacred and all-important that we find all the solutions to our problems? Can we not simply agree to disagree - with no love lost in the process?"; (c) "Face it - love is not the answer to everything - and sometimes not to anything!"

   FF: Acceptance, tolerance, emotional relief.

   GC: Because people are different they are likely to have boundary disputes. Negotiating compromises about these differences rather than lamenting the fact that they exist would seem like a better route to go.

26. IB: *To trust a loved one (especially if he or she has once betrayed your trust) is dangerous and fearsome; therefore you should be terribly concerned about it and keep dwelling on the worst possibility recurring.*

   FSS: "Betrayal is catastrophic. If I worry about it enough my concerns will show and prevent such an awesome event."

   IE: Worry, fear, high stress.

   CSS: (a) "Trusting myself enough to be able to stand on my own two feet in the event I would lose my mate makes it more convenient for me to trust him"; (b) "There is no magic; thinking does not make it so.

In fact, the more I fool myself into thinking I can use worry to head off what I foolishly believe would be disaster, the more likely I will assist in producing the results I wish to avoid"; (c) "If I lose him - he loses me!"

FF: Self-confidence, emotional independence, emotional relief.

GC: Mistrust of another is often rooted in insecurity, a mistrust of self. Minimizing fears of abandonment by trusting one's own emotional sustaining potential permits a more refreshing, concerned but not consumed perspective on the relationship.

Emotional dependency is not like a virus. It is neither caught from someone else nor cured by someone else. Some things cannot be done to or for another person. Tying and untying dependency knots is one of those items. Try to distinguish between love and dependency. Love is energizing, increases vitality, is in your best experiential interest, and allows you to let go when you sense the relationship is over. Dependency exhausts, drains, and saps you, and works against your best emotional interests. If you find you have put yourself in such an emotional straitjacket, decide to become your own physician and heal yourself from the faulty notions that you bind yourself with. Untie and unblock yourself from your rigid rules of loving, perhaps not helping yourself to ultimate emotional freedom - but certainly to making yourself to be easier and more enjoying in the relationship.

Bibliography

Alberti, R. E. (1990). *Stand Up, Speak Out, Talk Back.* San Luis
   Obispo, CA: Impact.
Bach, G. R., & Wyden, P. (1968). *The Intimate Enemy.* New
   York: Avon.
Becker, W. C. (1971). *Parents Are Teachers.* Champaign, IL:
   Research Press.
Bernard, M. E., & Joyce, M. R. (1984). *Rational-Emotive Therapy
   With Children and Adolescents.* New York: John Wiley and
   Sons.
Borcherdt, B. (1989). *Think Straight! Feel Great! 21 Guides to
   Emotional Self-Control.* Sarasota, FL: Professional Resource
   Exchange.
Borcherdt, B. (1993). *You Can Control Your Feelings! 24 Guides
   to Emotional Well-Being.* Sarasota, FL: Professional Re-
   source Press.
Dryden, W. (1990). *Dealing With Anger Problems: Rational-
   Emotive Therapeutic Interventions.* Sarasota, FL: Profes-
   sional Resource Exchange.
Dryden, W. (1991). *A Dialogue With Albert Ellis: Against
   Dogma.* Philadelphia, PA: Open University Press.
Dryden, W., & DiGiuseppe, R. (1990). *A Primer on Rational-
   Emotive Therapy.* San Jose, CA: Resource Press.
Dryden, W., & Golden, W. L. (1987). *Cognitive-Behavioral
   Approaches to Psychotherapy.* Bristol, PA: Hemisphere Pub-
   lishing.
Ellis, A. (1961). *A Guide to a Successful Marriage.* N. Holly-
   wood, CA: Wilshire Book Company.

Ellis, A. (1965). *Suppressed: 7 Key Essays Publishers Dared Not Print.* Chicago, IL: New Classics House.

Ellis, A. (1966). *The Art and Science of Love.* Secaucus, NJ: Lyle Stuart.

Ellis, A. (1972a). *The Civilized Couple's Guide to Extra-Marital Affairs.* New York: Peter H. Wyden.

Ellis, A. (1972b). *The Sensuous Person: Critique and Corrections.* Secaucus, NJ: Lyle Stuart.

Ellis, A. (1975). *How to Live With a Neurotic at Home and Work.* New York: Crown Publishers.

Ellis, A. (1979a). *The Intelligent Woman's Guide to Dating and Mating.* Secaucus, NJ: Lyle Stuart.

Ellis, A. (1979b). *Overcoming Procrastination.* New York: Signet.

Ellis, A. (1988). *How to Stubbornly Refuse to Make Yourself Miserable About Anything — Yes, Anything!* Secaucus, NJ: Lyle Stuart.

Ellis, A. (1991). *Why Am I Always Broke: How to be Sure About Money.* New York: Carol Publishing.

Ellis, A., & Becker, I. (1982). *A Guide to Personal Happiness.* N. Hollywood, CA: Wilshire Book Company.

Ellis, A., & Harper, R. (1975). *A New Guide to Rational Living.* N. Hollywood, CA: Wilshire Book Company.

Ellis, A., & Yeager, R. J. (1989). *Why Some Therapies Don't Work: The Dangers of Transpersonal Psychology.* Buffalo, NY: Prometheus Books.

Frankl, V. E. (1959). *Man's Search for Meaning.* New York: Touchstone Books.

Garcia, E. (1979). *Developing Emotional Muscle.* Atlanta: Author.

Garner, A. (1981). *Conversationally Speaking.* New York: McGraw-Hill.

Glasser, W. (1975). *Reality Therapy.* New York: Harper Colophon Books.

Greenberg, D. (1966). *How to Make Yourself Miserable.* New York: Random House.

Greiger, R. M., & Boyd, J. D. (1980). *Rational-Emotive Therapy: A Skills Based Approach*. New York: Van Nostrand Reinhold.

Grossack, M. (1976). *Love, Sex, and Self-Fulfillment*. New York: Signet.

Harris, S. (1982). *Pieces of Eight*. Boston: Houghton Mifflin.

Hauck, P. (1971). *Marriage Is a Loving Business*. Philadelphia, PA: The Westminster Press.

Hauck, P. (1974). *Overcoming Frustration and Anger*. Philadelphia, PA: The Westminster Press.

Hauck, P. (1976). *How to Do What You Want to Do*. Philadelphia, PA: The Westminster Press.

Hauck, P. (1981). *Overcoming Jealousy and Possessiveness*. Philadelphia, PA: The Westminster Press.

Hauck, P. (1984). *The Three Faces of Love*. Philadelphia, PA: The Westminster Press.

Hoffer, E. (1966). *The True Believer*. New York: Perennial Library.

Jourard, S. (1971). *The Transparent Self*. New York: D. Van Nostrand.

Lazarus, A. A. (1981). *The Practice of Multi-Modal Therapy*. New York: McGraw-Hill.

Lazarus, A. A. (1985). *Marital Myths: Two Dozen Mistaken Beliefs That Can Ruin a Marriage (or Make a Bad One Worse)*. San Luis Obispo, CA: Impact.

Lazarus, A. A. (1989). *The Practice of Multimodal Therapy: Systematic, Comprehensive and Effective Psychotherapy*. Baltimore, MD: Johns Hopkins.

Maultsby, M. (1975). *Help Yourself to Happiness*. New York: Institute for Rational Living.

Paterson, G. R. (1978). *Families*. Champaign, IL: Research Press.

Russell, B. (1971). *The Conquest of Happiness*. New York: Liveright.

Russianoff, P. (1983). *Why Do I Think I'm Nothing Without a Man?* New York: Bantam Books.

Satir, V. (1972). *Peoplemaking.* Palo Alto, CA: Science and Behavior Books.

Shedd, C. W. (1978). *Smart Dads I Know.* New York: Avon.

Simon, S. B. (1978). *Negative Criticism and What You Can Do About It.* Niles, IL: Argus Communications.

Smith, M. J. (1975). *When I Say No, I Feel Guilty.* New York: Bantam Books.

Walen, S. R., DiGiuseppe, R., & Wessler, R. L. (1980). *A Practitioner's Guide to Rational-Emotive Therapy.* New York: Oxford University Press.

Young, H. S. (1974). *A Rational Counseling Primer.* New York: Institute for Rational Living.

Zilbergeld, B. (1978). *Male Sexuality.* Boston, MA: Little, Brown, and Company.

Zilbergeld, B. (1983). *The Shrinking of America: Myths of Psychological Change.* Boston, MA: Little, Brown, and Company.

Zilbergeld, B. (1992). *The New Male Sexuality.* New York: Bantam Books.

If You Found This Book Useful . . .

You might want to know more about our other titles.

If you would like to receive our latest catalog, please return this form:

Name:_____
(Please Print)

Address:_____

Address:_____

City/State/Zip:_____

Telephone:(_____)_____

I am a:

_____ Psychologist   _____ Mental Health Counselor
_____ Psychiatrist   _____ Marriage and Family Therapist
_____ School Psychologist   _____ Not in Mental Health Field
_____ Clinical Social Worker   _____ Other:_____

◆   ◆   ◆

Professional Resource Press
P.O. Box 15560
Sarasota, FL 34277-1560

Telephone #941-366-7913
FAX #941-366-7971

HHL/2/96

Add A Colleague To Our Mailing List . . .

If you would like us to send our latest catalog to one of your colleagues, please return this form.

Name:_____
(Please Print)

Address:_____

Address:_____

City/State/Zip:_____

Telephone:(_____)_____

I am a:

_____ Psychologist   _____ Mental Health Counselor
_____ Psychiatrist   _____ Marriage and Family Therapist
_____ School Psychologist   _____ Not in Mental Health Field
_____ Clinical Social Worker   _____ Other:_____

◆   ◆   ◆

Professional Resource Press
P.O. Box 15560
Sarasota, FL 34277-1560

Telephone #941-366-7913
FAX #941-366-7971

HHL/2/96